STRESS INOCULATION TRAINING

Pergamon Titles of Related Interest

Blanchard/Andrasik MANAGEMENT OF CHRONIC HEADACHES:
A Psychological Approach

Farber STRESS AND BURNOUT IN THE HUMAN
SERVICE PROFESSIONS

Felner/Jason/Moritsugu/Farber PREVENTIVE PSYCHOLOGY:
Theory, Research and Practice

Hersen/Kazdin/Bellack THE CLINICAL
PSYCHOLOGY HANDBOOK

Holzman/Turk PAIN MANAGEMENT: A Handbook of Treatment
Approaches

Kanfer/Goldstein HELPING PEOPLE CHANGE: A Textbook of
Methods, Third Edition

Karoly/Jensen MULTIMETHOD ASSESSMENT OF
CHRONIC PAIN

Related Journals *

ADDICTIVE BEHAVIORS
BEHAVIORAL ASSESSMENT
CLINICAL PSYCHOLOGY REVIEW

*Free sample copies available upon request

PSYCHOLOGY PRACTITIONER GUIDEBOOKS

EDITORS

Arnold P. Goldstein, Syracuse University
Leonard Krasner, SUNY at Stony Brook
Sol. L. Garfield, Washington University

STRESS INOCULATION TRAINING

DONALD MEICHENBAUM
University of Waterloo

PERGAMON PRESS
New York   Oxford   Toronto   Sydney   Paris   Frankfurt

Pergamon Press Offices:

U.S.A.   Pergamon Press Inc., Maxwell House, Fairview Park,
                  Elmsford, New York 10523, U.S.A.

U.K.   Pergamon Press Ltd., Headington Hill Hall,
                  Oxford OX3 0BW, England

CANADA   Pergamon Press Canada Ltd., Suite 104, 150 Consumers Road,
                  Willowdale, Ontario M2J 1P9, Canada

AUSTRALIA   Pergamon Press (Aust.) Pty. Ltd., P.O. Box 544,
                  Potts Point, NSW 2011, Australia

FRANCE   Pergamon Press SARL, 24 rue des Ecoles,
                  75240 Paris, Cedex 05, France

FEDERAL REPUBLIC   Pergamon Press GmbH, Hammerweg 6,
OF GERMANY   D-6242 Kronberg-Taunus, Federal Republic of Germany

Library of Congress Cataloging in Publication Data

Meichenbaum, Donald.

 Stress inoculation training.

 (Psychology practitioner guidebooks)
 1. Stress (Psychology) – Prevention. 2. Behavior
therapy. 3. Cognitive therapy. I. Title. II. Series.
[DNLM: 1. Stress, Psychological – therapy. WM 172 M499s]
BF575.S75M455 1985   155.9   85-492
ISBN 0-08-031597-6
ISBN 0-08-031596-8 (pbk.)

Printed in Great Britain by A. Wheaton & Co. Ltd., Exeter

Dedicated to
those who have contributed to the
development of stress inoculation training,
and most importantly, to those who
will critically evaluate and develop
it further

Contents

Preface

One of the major growth industries in North America is that of books and workshops on stress reduction and prevention. These nostrums take one of two formats—they either advocate one specific stress management technique such as meditation, relaxation, and aerobic exercise, or they espouse an eclectic approach consisting of an array of techniques that usually includes relaxation (the "aspirin" of the stress reduction field), meditation and biofeedback training, drugs, cognitive approaches, time management procedures, dietary and life-style changes, and training in interpersonal assertiveness and value clarification. These procedures are usually offered in an atheoretical framework, and they convey the flavor that there is a "right" way to cope or adjust.

The object of this book is *not* to add to this array, but rather to provide an integrative framework for a better understanding and critique of current efforts designed to reduce and prevent maladaptive stress reactions. Moreover, the present book will present a clinical guide for a cognitive behavioral treatment procedure called Stress Inoculation Training (SIT).[1] During the last decade, my colleagues and I have been researching and clinically developing this comprehensive treatment intervention, which has been applied by many other investigators to a variety of diverse populations on both a treatment and a prevention basis.[2] This book will describe the clinical wisdom that has emerged from these efforts.

SIT is no panacea. Instead, it is a clinically sensitive, multileveled, multifaceted intervention that should be critically evaluated. My goals in writing this book are twofold. First, because the present period in the field of behavior change is characterized by therapists "going public" with their

[1]While the concept of "inoculation" will be considered in detail in chapter 3, at this point it is worth noting that the word *inoculation* (not *innoculation*) is one of the most misspelled words in the English language. I once considered writing an article entitled "Stress Inoculation Training, an *N* of One" (not including the final *n* at the end of the word).

[2]I am indebted to Dennis Turk, Roy Cameron, and Myles Genest, who have worked with me on the clinical development and on the conceptualization of stress inoculation training.

treatment manuals, I offer this book in that same spirit, with the hope that it will stimulate further critical evaluation (e.g., see Luborsky & De Rubeis, 1984). My second objective is to influence the "internal dialogue," that is, what clinicians or researchers will say to themselves the next time they see a stressed client, conduct a stress reduction workshop, write a book on stress reduction and prevention, or undertake research on stress management.

In order to achieve these objectives, the book has been organized into seven chapters. Chapter 1 considers the concepts of stress and coping from a transactional perspective, the role of cognitions and emotions in stress reactions, and the need to supplement person-oriented interventions with environment-oriented interventions. Once one has an appreciation of the conceptual model underlying the present approach, then the specific SIT treatment procedures will make more sense. The various interventions will *not* appear to be a hodgepodge of clinical techniques but a logical sequence following from a collaborative analysis with clients or participants. As Kendall and Bemis (1983) observed:

> Stress inoculation training [SIT] appears to be the most inclusive form of cognitive-behavioral therapy surveyed. . . . [SIT] reflects a deliberate plan with a plausible underlying rationale. . . . [SIT] presents a range of strategies from among which the most appealing and efficacious can be selected. In this way the client can serve as a collaborator in helping to generate an individually tailored coping package suited to his or her own needs and experiences. (p. 580)

Chapter 2 briefly considers a set of clinical guidelines for conducting stress reduction and prevention programs. These guidelines derive from a review of the major findings in the areas of stress research and behavior change. A major concern in this and subsequent chapters will be the issue of client resistance and treatment nonadherence. All too often the focus of clinical guidebooks is on the "how–to" features of an intervention, and little or no effort is expended on how one "hooks" (motivates for change) the client, significant others, an organization, or a social agency. This chapter considers various ways in which the trainer can anticipate and subsume possible resistance and reactions to setbacks into the training regimen (i.e., the issue of relapse prevention).

In chapter 3, the SIT regimen is described, considering the variety of populations to which it has been applied on both a preventative and treatment basis. SIT consists of three phases: the conceptualization phase, the skills acquisition and rehearsal phase, and the application and follow-through phase. Chapters 4, 5, and 6 describe each of these phases, respectively. Although the three phases of SIT are described sequentially, they constitute a highly flexible, interdependent, multifaceted training regimen. They are *not* a loose compendium of unrelated methods, but rather a set of interconnnected interventions that can be combined in a systematic way. The three phases are lock-keyed, and training often involves the recycling of the respective phases or overlap, depending upon the time frame and the specific population.

The final chapter illustrates some of the ways that SIT has been applied to a variety of different populations and settings such as medical patients, nurses, police officers, schoolteachers, athletes, and, finally, victims of major life-stressful events. In each of these cases, some preliminary data have been provided for the promising potential of applying SIT to non-clinical and clinical populations. SIT remains at an early stage of development, and it has not yet been fully systematically evaluated. The present book is designed to nurture and further stimulate such clinical and research efforts.

Chapter 1

Conceptual Model Underlying Stress Inoculation Training

There are many different ways to introduce the conceptual model underlying SIT. One such method is to employ a personal anecdote of a stressful event. Because stressors come in various forms including cataclysmic events, personal loss, and daily hassles, the present anecdote falls into the last category, namely, recurrent social frictions, often of our own making. I offer this anecdote for the following three reasons:

1. I enjoy telling this vignette because many other people can readily identify with it.
2. I analyze the anecdote in order to illustrate the transactional nature of stress and coping and how one can conceptualize the role of cognitions in stress reactions.
3. Finally, I suspect that, when you have completed this book, what you will recall most are my anecdotes, which may have elicited affect (e.g., humor or anger). It is to be hoped that such anecdotes will act as a retrieval cue for the recall of relevant content. If indeed this is true, then I would argue that this fact has important implications for how we conduct training. What is it that clients take away from our training sessions? How should we use humor, self-disclosure, and the like in treatment and training? Can we use metaphors and anecdotes to help clients retrieve information and cope more effectively in their daily lives? We will consider these questions further in chapter 5.

The anecdote I am about to describe conveys what I call "instant chaos," and it grows out of our current research project on parental stress. Those of you who have children of your own will be able to readily identify with this anecdote. Those readers who do not have children can look upon this anecdote as a vicarious trial in stress inoculation training or as a birth control device, whichever is more appropriate.

As the father of four children and as a clinical psychologist interested in anger control, I have become very interested in the topic of child abuse. My approach to this topic is somewhat different from that of other investigators. Simply put, I am interested in learning why the incidence of child abuse is not higher. Not that it is underreported per se, but, instead, the question arises: What are "normal" parents doing to control their anger and aggression in handling the stress of parenting? Consider the following incident:

> My wife went out for the evening, and it was my job to give my four children (ages 2 to 10) dinner, which she had prepared, and then to go through "the ritual," namely, give baths, help with homework, read bedtime stories, and participate in related activities that come with the territory of being a father.
>
> I began by making an error. On this particular evening I had hoped to watch a special television program that began at 9:00. I don't watch television very often, but on this evening there was something on that I really wanted to see. The mistake, as will become evident, was the incompatibility of having a hidden agenda or plan and having four children. Hidden agendas and children are often incompatible events and, in retrospect, I can see I was setting myself up for potential stress.
>
> The evening's events began rather pleasantly as I gave my youngest son, Danny, a bath after dinner—a most delightful and enjoyable time for both father and son. During the course of the bath, my eldest daughter, Lauren, appeared on the scene and innocently asked, "Dad, could you help me find my ruler?" My reaction was to encourage independence training, posing questions about where she had seen the ruler last and so on. (Lauren's request for the ruler will take on more significance as the anecdote unfolds.) So far, so good!
>
> With the 2-year-old in bed, the next task was to see that 4-year-old David had a bath. Fortunately, 8-year-old Michelle volunteered to give David a bath, an invitation I readily accepted. While I was cleaning up in the kitchen, a "critical stimulus event" occurred. I heard David running in the tub and from years of experience I had a flood of catastrophizing thoughts, images, and accompanying feelings. "Oh, no, not again. Remember how he fell the last time. How many times have I told him?" With images of impending disaster and feelings of foreboding, I raced up the stairs to stop David. As I opened the bathroom door, the doorknob smashed into the eye of Michelle, who was drying herself. "Oh no, what have I done?"
>
> David was completely immune to these goings-on and continued to run in the tub. In a controlled-anger fashion (that is, loud enough to get him to stop, but supposedly not loud enough to wake up his sleeping brother), I exhorted David to stop. At which point David became startled and did indeed fall, swallowing water and beginning to choke. Given David's past history with croup, my sense of alarm was now heightened.
>
> At this point, a crying Danny awoke, followed by Lauren's reappearance on the scene to innocently ask if I had found her ruler yet. "What, your ruler! Don't you see what has happened? Instant chaos has broken out!"

As I mentioned, anyone who is a parent has likely experienced many similar situations. As parents know, you sort these things out. You put ice on Michelle's eye, you put Danny back to bed, you comfort David, and you never find Lauren's ruler. By this time it is 9:15 and you decide to collapse in front of the television set with a palliative coping device in your hand (a glass of Scotch).

At which point Michelle calls down for a drink (of grape juice!), which usually ends the nighttime ritual. In order to be efficient, I decided to take the drink up to her bedroom, feeling bad about what I had done to her. Unfortunately, she spilled the juice all over herself and the mattress, and I looked at the mess and wondered why the incidence of child abuse isn't higher. I immediately developed empathy for single parents, who have to deal with such crises alone. At least I knew that my wife would be returning soon, and I could tell her what *her* children had done to me that evening.

This anecdote can be analyzed at several levels, each of which will help us better understand the transactional nature of stress and coping. The concept of stress has been used in many different ways. Some investigators have defined stress as a condition of the environment (e.g., stress of work, of competition, or of raising children). According to this view, stress reflects a set of external forces impinging upon the individual or the group. Another view of stress relates to the individual's response when placed in a challenging or threatening environment. Here we are referring to the individual's or group's psychological and physiological reaction when exposed to a challenging environment.

In the present context, stress is viewed as neither a stimulus nor a response, but rather as the result of a *transaction*, influenced by both the individual and the environment. From a transactional perspective, stress is defined as a cognitively mediated relational concept. It reflects the relationship between the person and the environment that is appraised by the person as taxing or exceeding his or her resources and as endangering his or her well-being. As Folkman (1984) noted, stress is not the property of the person or the environment, nor is it a stimulus or a response. Stress is a particular dynamic relationship (constantly changing and bidirectional) between the person and the environment as they act on each other. As Lazarus (1981) commented, individuals are not mere victims of stress, but how they appraise stressful events (primary appraisal) and how they appraise their coping resources and options (secondary appraisal) determine the nature of stress. The individual's appraisal processes influence the dynamic relationship or transaction between the individual and the social environment. In this context, coping refers to behavioral and cognitive efforts to master, reduce, or tolerate the internal and/or external demands that are created by stressful transactions (Lazarus & Folkman, 1984).

The transactional model emphasizes the cognitive interpersonal context of stress. Often, stressed individuals or groups inadvertently create and engender reactions in others that maintain maladaptive stress responses. The very method intended to solve problems often ends up intensifying them. Many examples could be given of stressed individuals who become fearful, avoidant, depressed, angered, and so forth and who engender in others reactions that serve to maintain such maladaptive stress patterns. For example, stressed individuals who become fearful and avoidant could elicit overprotectiveness from others, resulting in the first person's not testing out his or her concerns and fears, which in turn breeds further lack of self-confidence. Such avoidance leads to further overprotectiveness, strengthening the vicious cycle. A built-in self-confirmatory process emerges as clients appraise (selectively attend, recall, and encode) events as being consistent with their biases or schemas. In this way, individuals play a critical role in defining stress.

We can illustrate this transactional perspective by analyzing my anecdote of putting my four children to bed. In this situation, I was not merely the victim of stress, but I played an active role in contributing to the stress I experienced. How I behaved, how I appraised events, my thoughts, my images, and my feelings each contributed to the stress reactions I experienced. I inadvertently contributed to and engendered the stressful situation. All too often our clients behave in a similar fashion, not realizing the sequence of events by which they help to create and maintain the very stressful reactions they complain about. It is the task of SIT to enlist clients as collaborators in collecting data that will lead to their recognizing low-intensity cues and their learning to interrupt and change such stress-engendering behavioral patterns. Chapter 4 considers the specific clinical techniques and ploys that can be used to establish such a collaborative relationship. For now, let us more fully analyze the anecdote of putting my four children to bed.

THE ROLE OF BEHAVIOR

Let's begin at the level of behavior. The trainer usually begins by interviewing the client, in order to assess the adequacy of his or her behavioral repertoire. Is the individual stressed because he or she lacks the interpersonal or parental skills that would help to avoid or reduce stress? The clinician or trainer might ask, "Don, if I watched you put your children to bed what would I see and hear?" In this way the trainer tries to ascertain the variety of available coping responses. Does this parent tend to scream, yell, or hit, or does he use reasoning, humor, and affection to achieve his goals? The trainer might wish to supplement such self-reports with direct observation in the home and in the clinic and to secure reports from significant others (spouse, children).

Moreover, the trainer might define the nature of the client's behavioral repertoire in its broadest sense, going beyond observable behavior to include the knowledge and expectations the parent has about children's behavior. For example, Twentyman and his colleagues (Twentyman, Rohrbeck, & Amish, 1984) indicate that abusive parents often have unrealistic expectations and inadequate knowledge of child behaviors.

THE ROLE OF OTHERS

We know, however, that, not only do parents affect their children, but we are also dealing with a bidirectional process of children affecting parents. In order to understand the nature of someone's report of stress, a trainer needs to go beyond the client and appreciate the impact of significant others as well as environmental milieus and organizational and societal agencies. To understand the stress I experienced in putting my four children to bed, I need to assess the interpersonal and the intrapersonal consequences (i.e., my feelings and thoughts) that followed my efforts.

This need to assess the impact of children on parents is nicely illustrated in an ongoing research project in which we asked parents to describe an instance of when they were stressed in handling their children. For example, one parent reported being terribly upset with his 10-year-old son, whom he was going to severely reprimand. As the father opened the door to the boy's bedroom he saw his son standing at attention playing "Taps" (a tune to commemorate the dead) on his trumpet. This stopped the father in his tracks, and broad smiles appeared on both their faces. The son had used humor to interrupt and de-escalate the stressful interaction. This anecdote indicates not only that the father was stressed, but also that, more importantly, the father's stressful reaction was open to interruption. Instead of viewing the son's efforts as further provocation ("I'll take that trumpet and wrap it around your head. Don't try to weasel out of this one"), the father viewed the son's behavior as an engaging way to handle a stressful situation. How the father appraised the son's behavior was critical in determining the nature of the stressful transaction. It is not only that we are stressed, but it is also how open we are to interruption and how we rebound from stressful situations that seem critical to the ability to cope.

The object of any stress management training program is not to encourage participants to eliminate stress. As Selye (1974) noted, life would be boring without the challenge of stressful situations. Instead, the goal of training should be to educate clients about the nature and impact of stress and to ensure that they have the variety of intrapersonal and interpersonal skills to use stress constructively. Becoming angry with one's children is a normal human reaction, and there is nothing wrong in expressing such feelings. Our concern is that such anger might translate into uncontrollable aggression. No matter how effective a stress management program is, it is highly likely that clients will have a recurrence or encounter setbacks (reexperience anger, pain, depression, parental stress). As we will see, one goal of SIT is to influence how clients respond (appraise, interrupt, and produce adaptive coping reactions) given such recurrences.

THE ROLE OF COGNITION

The stress I experienced in putting my children to bed was influenced not only by what I did and by the consequences that followed, but also by the thoughts, images, and feelings I experienced before, during, and after the incident. Because the nature of my thoughts played such an important role in influencing my stress, it is useful to consider the role of cognition in more detail. We can distinguish three different ways in which the concept of cognition is used, namely, as cognitive events, as cognitive processes, and as cognitive structures. Let us consider each briefly; then we can examine their role in stress reactions.

Cognitive events refer to conscious, identifiable thoughts and images. They occur in the individual's stream of consciousness, or they can usually be readily retrieved upon request. Beck (1976) has described these as automatic thoughts—discrete messages that appear in shorthand form, are almost always unquestioned and believed, are experienced as spontaneous, are often couched in terms of *should*, *ought*, or *must*, are relatively idiosyncratic, and are difficult to turn off. As Beck noted,

> The person perceives these thoughts as though they are by reflex—without any reflection or reasoning, and they impress him or her as plausible and valid. (1976, p. 237)

Meichenbaum (1977) has described such cognitive events as a form of internal dialogue that takes place when the automaticity of one's behavior is interrupted. This dialogue incorporates, among other things, attributions, expectations, and evaluations of self and/or task or task-irrelevant thoughts and images.

It should be noted, however, that it is not as if people go about talking to themselves. Instead, they usually behave in a "mindless" and scripted fashion. However, under certain conditions, conscious processes can come into play. For example, when individuals have to exercise choice or judgments, as in uncertain or novel situations or when they must weigh possible outcomes and consequences, they tend to talk to themselves.

Prior to treatment, however, it is unlikely that clients monitor their thoughts, images, and feelings consciously or deliberately when facing stressful situations. Rather, as Goldfried, Decenteceo, and Weinberg (1974) have indicated, because of the habitual nature of one's expectations and beliefs, it is likely that such thinking processes become automatic and seemingly involuntary, like most overlearned acts. The client's negative, stress-engendering, internal dialogue becomes a habitual style of thinking, in many ways similar to the automatization of thought that accompanies the mastery of a motor skill such as driving a car or skiing. Nevertheless, the trainer can help a client become aware of such thought processes and increase the likelihood that in the future he or she will notice and change this internal dialogue. In some instances, the client's cognitive events might take a pictorial as well as a verbal form.

The nature and content of such cognitive events can influence how one feels and behaves. As Sarason (1975) has noted, individuals under stress tend to become self-preoccupied, often displaying a variety of self-defeating and interfering thoughts and feelings. Engaging in such self-defeating thoughts and feelings is likely to lead to less than optimal performance, further increasing an already high level of emotional and behavioral dysfunction. The notion of cognitive events is consistent with Richard Lazarus's (1981) and John Mason's (1975) views that the degree to which a particular situation elicits an emotional response depends in large part on the organism's appraisal of the situation and his or her ability to handle the event. As Beck (1984) noted, stress-prone individuals are primed to make extreme, one-sided, absolutistic, categorical, global judgments. They tend to personalize events and engage in cognitive distortions such as polarization (black-white dichotomous reasoning), magnification and exaggeration (overemphasis on the most negative possibilities in a given situation), and overgeneralization. Such conceptual distortions can occur in an automatic, unconscious fashion.

A second way in which the concept of cognition is used is called *cognitive processes*. This term refers to the way we automatically or unconsciously process information including search and storage mechanisms, inferential and retrieval processes. These processes shape mental representations and schemata. Personal knowledge of such cognitive processes and the ability to control them represent metacognition, which provides an interface between that which is normally out of conscious awareness and that which is accessible to assessment, research, and training.

Under most circumstances we do not attend to how we appraise situations, how we selectively attend and recall events, how we selectively seek information that is consistent with our beliefs. Several different cognitive processes have been described including mental heuristics à la Tversky and Kahneman (1977), metacognition à la Flavell (1979), and self-confirmatory bias à la Frank (1974). These cognitive processes have been described in detail by Meichenbaum and Gilmore (1984), Nisbett and Ross (1980), Taylor and Crocker (1981), and Turk and Speers (1983). The cognitive process that has most relevance for SIT training is that of *confirmatory bias*, or a self-fulfilling process. We selectively perceive, remember, and interpret experience so as to filter out disconfirmations. Mahoney (1982) described the process by which the individual tends to select and process stimuli that are congruent as *feed forward*. As one seeks and then confirms one's beliefs, those beliefs (schemata) become even more active. For instance, individuals who are preoccupied with concerns of equity are likely to scan their environment for signs of potential injustice and to misread events as personal slights. Such appraisal can lead to interpersonal consequences that confirm the client's concerns. In this way, the notions of fairness become progressively more dominant. Such cognitive schemata become prepotent and activate particular emotional and behavioral tendencies.

Snyder (1981) has described how one's untested assumptions can lead to behavior that engenders reactions in others that in turn confirm one's maladaptive beliefs. In this way, a self-defeating cycle is created and perpetuated. This "seek and ye shall find" phenomenon is nicely illustrated in a study by Kelley and Stahelski (1970), who found that subjects who imagined others to be very competitive consequently behaved competitively toward them. This in turn elicited competitive counterresponses that confirmed their competitiveness view of the world. Thus, one's initial assumption acts as a self-fulfilling prophecy. Many clinical examples of this process could be offered. For instance, the depressed individual may confirm his or her own hypothesized undesirableness by defensive social behavior that contributes to social rejection. Such social rejection is in turn taken as proof of his or her initial assumption of low personal self-worth. Stressed individuals often engender responses in others that confirm their maladaptive beliefs. Such a confirmatory bias has important implications for the role of relapse prevention in SIT. Clients have a penchant for interpreting setbacks as confirmation of their bias of being unable to cope or handle stress. As we shall see, SIT anticipates and incorporates such possible reactions to setbacks into the training regimen.

Finally, the term *cognitive structures* refers to the tacit assumptions, beliefs, commitments, and meanings that influence habitual ways of construing oneself and the world. Cognitive structures can be thought of as schemata that are implicit or operate at an unconscious level, are highly interdependent, and probably are hierarchically arranged. Schemata are mental organizations of experience that influence the way information is processed and the way behavior is organized. Cognitive structures may engender cognitive and affective processes and events and may in turn be developed or modified by ongoing processes and events. As Taylor and Crocker (1981) noted, cognitive structures or schemata serve several purposes including helping individuals identify stimuli quickly, categorize them in appropriate units, fill in missing information, select a strategy for obtaining further information, solve a problem, and reach a goal. Schemata serve encoding and representational functions as well as interpretative and inferential functions.

Markus (1977) has demonstrated that such schemata can extend to information about oneself, influencing what stimuli are attended to, how they are structured, what importance is attached to them, and what happens subsequently. For instance, clients might see themselves as inadequate or unlovable; they might see others as domineering or exploitative. Given such a cognitive set, clients might handicap themselves by misreading situations, avoiding opportunities, or behaving in a maladaptive fashion.

Stressful life events can trigger such schemata. Beck (1984) has viewed such schemas as specific sensitive areas or specific emotional vulnerabilities that result in individuals' predilections to overreact. Such hypersensitivities or cognitive structures act as templates that influence the way situations are appraised and that guide cognitive-affective processes and behavior. Cognitive structures operate as "latent perceptual readiness programs," priming individuals to respond in certain ways. Neisser (1976) described such cognitive structures as being analogous to format statements addressed to a computer. Meichenbaum and Gilmore (1984) have noted the parallel between cognitive structures and Klinger's (1977; Klinger, Barta, & Maxeiner, 1981) notion of current concerns and the psychodynamic notion of personal themes that exert their influence across situations (Strupp & Binder, 1982; Wachtel, 1977, 1982).

Change in one's cognitive structures is most likely to occur by discovering through enactive experience that old cognitive structures are questioned and unwarranted and that the adoption of new, more adaptive, structures is rewarding. The data of experience (i.e., the results of personal experiments) provide the most convincing basis for reconstruing one's self, the world, and the commerce between the two.

If we go back to the situation of putting my children to bed, we can identify the role that cognitive events, processes, and structures played in a stressful reaction. In order to tap the content of my cognitive events, I could close my eyes and imagine the scene and share with you, the reader, the thoughts, images, and feelings that preceded, accompanied, and followed the incident. (We will consider this imagery reconstruction procedure in detail in chapter 4.) The "catastrophizing" images I had upon hearing my son David run in the tub, the automatic thoughts I had about being overwhelmed, and so forth, conveyed the cognitive events I experienced.

The nature of cognitive structures can be conveyed by asking what about the situation of putting the children to bed caused me to become so stressed? Do I have specific concerns about issues of control or about equity and fairness? To answer this question, one can perform a situational analysis and consider which other situations are similarly stressful. Where else do I have similar thoughts and feelings? What is common across these situations? Do certain commonalities or themes emerge as I juxtapose these various stressful encounters? Do particular schemata (current concerns) characterize each? Am I more prone to appraise certain events, even ambiguous situations, in certain ways, thus contributing to my own stress level? In short, what is the nature of the cognitive structures that I carry with me that influence the content of my cognitive events and the nature of my cognitive processes? As we will see, SIT is designed to enlist clients in a collaborative relationship in trying to answer these questions. SIT helps clients become aware of the transactional nature of stress and coping, of how their reactions can contribute to and help maintain their stress reactions. In this way, the clients or participants can come to see the transactional perspective that underlies the SIT training.

GOING BEYOND THE INDIVIDUAL

The transactional perspective, however, requires that attempts at stress reduction and prevention go beyond the client, or for that matter, beyond the group. A transactional model of stress highlights the influence of both the individual *and* the environment. In many instances, attempts at stress reduction and prevention must go beyond teaching or nurturing problem-focused and palliative coping skills in clients. Often group, environmental, and organizational changes are required, and clients need to develop and employ direct-action behaviors to change their environments. A few examples will highlight the need for stress management training to go beyond the individual or the group.

For instance, SIT has been employed with rape victims, to help them deal with the trauma of such aggressive assaults. But such treatment would be short-sighted and relatively ineffective if it did not also consider needed changes in how various "helping" agencies (police, courts, the medical profession) inadvertently engender further stress in rape victims. These agencies' attitudes and behaviors toward the rape victim often foster a process of secondary victimization and further exacerbate the stress reaction. There is a need to educate and change the attitudes and behaviors of such agencies.

Similarly, SIT has been applied to medical patients about to undergo surgery or noxious medical examinations. As shown in chapter 7, providing information for and nurturing coping skills in medical patients is helpful, but a closely related complementary effort involves examining how the hospital implements policies that could engender further stress.

Two other examples will further underscore the need to supplement SIT training and extend it beyond the individual or the group. SIT has been applied to help athletes deal with the stress of competition, as described in chapter 7. Smoll and Smith (1980) have described the stress reduction value of also influencing the nature of the interactions between coaches and athletes. One can work with athletes by teaching them coping skills, but one can also try to influence the ways in which coaches interact with them.

Similarly, in the work environment there is a need not only to teach workers more efficient coping strategies, but also to help both management and workers consider organizational changes and job redesign. The object of stress management training should not be to help workers adapt to a noxious working environment. For instance, although SIT has been applied to helping police develop more effective ways of controlling anger and reducing stress, a complementary stress reduction intervention has been to have police choose and control their work schedules (i.e., choose rotation duties of day or night shifts). Similarly, Novaco, Cook, and Sarason (1983) reported how they successfully reduced stress among military recruits by going beyond the individual and establishing positive morale at the group level.

If we go back to my example of parental stress, stress reduction and prevention programs can be directed at helping parents further develop parenting skills. One can also consider how government, business, and social agencies can develop family support systems to reduce parental stress.

Stress reduction and prevention programs should go beyond teaching individuals specific coping skills. They should embrace the full significance of a transactional perspective. The individual, the environment, and the transaction between the two define and determine stress, and thus need to be the focus of assessment and change.

SUMMARY

In this chapter, the transactional perspective of stress and coping that underlies SIT was considered. It highlighted the role that cognitive events, processes, and structures play in stress reactions and the need for in-

terventions to go beyond the level of the individual. Subsequent chapters
consider how the SIT trainer enlists clients as collaborators in collecting
data, whereby they come to see their own contributions to their stress reactions. It is to be hoped that the specific assessment and training techniques
described will make more sense now that the conceptual model underlying SIT has been presented. You will see how the trainer taps the client's
cognitive events, searches with the client for cognitive structures, and
reveals the influence of cognitive processes. Such increased self-awareness
is viewed as a necessary but insufficient step in contributing to behavioral
change. The SIT trainer nurtures and teaches clients and participants a
variety of intrapersonal and interpersonal coping responses that they can
use to change their environment and control their reactions. Before we
consider specific SIT techniques, let us first review some clinical guidelines that should be followed in any stress reduction and prevention
program.

Chapter 2
Clinical Guidelines for Stress Prevention and Reduction Programs

As noted in the preface, the field of stress management is marked by the teaching of specific coping skills (e.g., relaxation and assertiveness) to target populations. Such an approach is understandable but somewhat problematic, given our limited knowledge about the nature of stress and coping. It is possible that the trainer might encourage clients to embrace and employ a specific coping technique when what is required is an entirely different mode of coping. In some stressful situations, retreat, toleration, disengagement, or even denial might be the most adaptive response. Training clients in reality testing, problem solving, and assertiveness could exacerbate stressful reactions (Lazarus, 1984).

Another way to voice this concern is to frame it in the form of a question. Having worked with impulsive children for a number of years, I have often wondered what happens to them when they grow up. My tongue-in-cheek answer is that they grow up and become mental health workers who conduct stress management workshops and who write "cookbooks" on how to cope. Like impulsive children, mental health professionals often intervene before they understand the nature of the problem. Moreover, the training program that is developed usually emphasizes the how-to features of the regimen and rarely considers how one prepares clients for intervention, how one motivates them to change, and how one deals with issues of resistance, nonadherence, and relapse. To combat such impulsive tendencies, the present chapter considers several guidelines that should be followed in developing, implementing, and evaluating stress management programs.

CLINICAL GUIDELINES

Careful Analysis

First, it is necessary to conduct a careful analysis of what has to be trained. This seems obvious, but, surprisingly, it is often overlooked. What

13

is the range of problems and challenges that confront the target population? What are the varieties of intrapersonal and interpersonal, group and societal responses that can be employed to cope effectively with the identified stressors? In answering these questions, it is important to keep in mind that the various indicators of coping (e.g., social functioning, positive mood, vocational adjustment, physiological symptoms) do not usually correlate highly.

As Cohen (1984) has aptly noted, there is no one-to-one relationship between the use of any one form of coping and adaptational outcome. What may be associated with positive outcomes under one set of circumstances may lead to negative outcomes under different circumstances. The point in time, the context and the outcome domain examined might each influence the adaptational value of the coping response. The relative efficacy of a specific coping response might be influenced by which measures one surveys (social, psychological, physiological) and whether one is looking at outcome in the short run or in the long run. What might be useful immediately might not be beneficial at a later time or in a different context. Simply put, the relationship among stress, coping, and outcome measures is complex, and this should give caution to those who set up stress management programs. For example, interventions that are designed to influence life-style, such as Type A behavior, may reduce the physiological risk of developing coronary heart disease, but may also influence personal and social behaviors that the individual and group find rewarding. Thus, trainers must be sensitive to all domains and should be cautious in considering the total health of individuals (Cohen, 1984).

In other words, a book on stress management should follow, not precede, research that has determined the usefulness of specific coping mechanisms. For example, Wortman (1983), in a very thoughtful article, noted that, for many mental health workers and the lay public, keeping one's emotional distress within manageable limits is frequently regarded as reflecting good adjustment in victims of stressful life events. Thus, stress management programs could be designed to help clients avoid emotional expression. However, in some instances, research has indicated that being actively upset with one's disability (e.g., spinal cord injuries, tuberculosis, cancer), or with having given birth to a malformed infant was more adaptive in the long run than restraining one's emotions (Cohen, 1984; Wortman, 1983). Similarly, Wortman reviewed research on the fact that maintaining a positive attitude or adopting a realistic approach to the situation is not always the most adaptive coping response.

Research findings such as these raise particular difficulties for those who wish to develop stress management programs. What should one train when the most adaptive coping mechanisms are not clear? There is not much normative information available to suggest how people should react to crises after varying lengths of time. Moreover, as Wortman noted, in many instances, life crises or being a victim can be conceptualized as a series of distinct coping tasks that can change over time as the crisis unfolds. Each task might require different coping responses. Each stress exposure sets off a process of adaptation that unfolds over time. This complexity and our basic ignorance of the mechanisms and factors involved should be a warning to would-be trainers of stress management. Moreover, it should encourage trainers to:

1. Be cautious in proposing any specific coping technique.
2. Be frank, open, and honest with clients in telling them what is and is not known.
3. Enlist clients as collaborators in determining the most useful coping approaches.
4. Be flexible in individually tailoring the coping training regimen to clients' specific situations and capabilities.
5. Adopt an analytic assessment approach to determine what needs to be trained.

Goldfried and D'Zurilla (1969) and Turk, Meichenbaum, and Genest (1983) have described such a behavior-analytic assessment approach consisting of three stages (problem identification, response enumeration, and response evaluation) that can be employed in the development of a stress management program. To reiterate, before we intervene, we must first analyze what it is that needs to be trained and what are the appropriate levels of intervention. One should assess the client's and the environment's strengths and determine if specific factors (e.g., maladaptive thoughts and feelings or a spouse-sabotaging program) interfere with implementation of already existing coping skills.

Diversity and Flexibility

Closely related to the need to "think before we act" is the recognition that any stress management training program must be diverse and flexible. This guideline derives from the observation that coping is neither a single act nor a static process. As Lazarus (1981) noted, coping is a constellation of many acts that stretch over time and undergo change. What could be a useful coping technique at one time might not be as useful at another time. Or for that matter, what might prove useful for one type of stressors or for one population might not be relevant on other occasions. For example, Pearlin and Schooler (1978) found that specific types of coping strategies are more or less effective depending upon the type of stress being faced. Coping strategies involving commitment and engagement with others were most effective in dealing with stressors arising in close interpersonal relations. In contrast, cognitive manipulations that distanced the person from the problem were most effective for stressors in economic and occupational areas. Different stressors call for different coping responses. Individuals may have to learn strategies to cope with specific situations. Thus, a stress management program should nurture a flexible coping repertoire. As Cohen (1984) states, "The key question may not be *which* coping strategies an individual uses but rather *how many* are in his or her repertoire or how flexible the person is in employing different strategies" (p. 269).

In some instances, the most effective coping responses directly address the problem, and, at other times, they focus on alleviating the emotional distress aroused by the problem. Lazarus and Folkman (1984) described two functions of coping: (a) *problem-focused coping*—designed to manage the problem causing the distress, and (b) *emotion-focused coping*—designed to regulate emotions or distress. In situations that are appraised as potentially changeable, problem-focused forms of coping (information gathering, problem solving, decision making, direct action) are more likely to be used. In stressful situations that are perceived as basically unchangeable, coping strategies are more likely to involve compromise, acceptance, and perhaps even distortion or denial (e.g., wish fulfillment). In such instances, emotion-focused coping can be used to alter the meaning of a situation. In many instances, individuals employ combinations of both problem-focused and emotion-focused coping. Thus, a stress-management program should nurture skills in both arenas.

Sensitivity to Individual Needs

Training must be sensitive to individual and cultural differences. As Silver and Wortman (1980) noted, people do *not* go through predictable and orderly reactions following stressful events. Therefore, interventions must be individually tailored. In terms of formulating training programs, it is important to remember that it is difficult to prepare individuals for unfamiliar experiences. Thus, there is a need to have trainees actively engage in stressful situations by means of role playing, imagery rehearsal, graded in vivo exposure, and so forth, so that they can learn how to cope step by step.

Given the marked variability of reactions to stressful events, stress training programs should take into consideration cultural differences in determining adaptive coping mechanisms. Attempting to train clients to cope in ways that violate cultural norms could actually aggravate stress-related problems. In some cultures, people tend to cope with stressors passively, by trying to endure them rather than viewing them as challenges and problems to be solved. Stress management training must reflect these cultural preferences.

Fostering Flexibility

Stress management programs should foster flexibility in a client's repertoire. Training programs should *not* foster a single or simple formula or a cookbook approach for coping with stress. The individual must learn to adjust his or her coping style to situational demands and changing contexts and goals.

Cognitive and Affective Factors

Stress management programs must recognize the important role that cognitive and affective factors play in determining what is stressful and the nature of the coping response. The individual's appraisal processes involving the magnitude of the stressor, the likelihood that it will occur, and the coping resources available to deal with it have a strong influence on the person's emotional reactions and choice of coping strategies (Lazarus & Folkman, 1984). Training programs that influence individuals' appraisals of stressors and coping resources will prove most effective. The trainer should establish a working relationship with clients, to make them feel comfortable disclosing their feelings and thoughts about stressful experiences and any concerns they have about the training program.

Graded Exposure

Exposure during training to less threatening stressors can potentiate new skills, enhance feelings of self-efficacy, and psychologically "immunize" the individual or the group. As Orne (1965) noted,

> One way of enabling an individual to become more resistant to stress is to allow him to have appropriate prior experience with the stimulus involved. The biological notion of immunization provides such a model. If an individual is given the opportunity to deal with a stimulus that is mildly stressful, he is able to do so successfully (mastering it in a psychological sense), he will tend to be able to tolerate similar stimulus of somewhat greater intensity in the future. . . . It would seem that one can markedly affect an individual's tolerance of stress by manipulating his beliefs about his performance in the situation . . . and his feelings that he can control his behavior. (pp. 315–316)

Such stress inoculation and graded exposure can engender a client's sense of self-confidence, hope, perceived control, commitment, and personal responsibility.

Direct Instruction

The training must provide direct instruction in generalization, as part of the intervention. The participants must receive "informed training," in which they are made fully aware of the rationale for training; are helped to collaborate in the development, implementation, and evaluation of coping procedures; and are reminded of how and why coping strategies can be of help. Generalization, or the application of coping skills to a variety of settings, should be actively planned and should be made part and parcel of the total training regimen. One cannot assume that generalization will follow from interventions. Instead, it must be explicitly trained. The likelihood of generalization will be enhanced if the training tasks are similar to the criterion situation.

Anticipating the Future

The training should be future-oriented, anticipating possible setbacks and future stressful life events. The client's thoughts and feelings surrounding failure are critical in determining whether setbacks lead to deterioration (feelings of "learned helplessness") or persistence (mastery orientation or feelings of "learned resourcefulness"). Does the client view such possible setbacks as inevitable and insurmountable, or does the client see lapses and backsliding as rectifiable and previous successes as replicable? The nature of the client's cognitions, in particular attributions about failure, plays a critical role in determining the pattern of reactions. Failure and further stress are likely to recur if clients attribute such setbacks to stable unchangeable factors and if they engage in characterological self-blame. Attributing failure to less stable factors such as insufficient effort, incorrect strategy, or bad luck implies that future success remains possible (Weiner, 1972). A stress management program must be sensitive to the client's future reactions to setbacks and should include relapse prevention in the training regimen. The trainer should anticipate and incorporate possible failures into the training regimen as described in chapter 5. In this way clients can identify high-risk situations in which they might encounter setbacks and thus prepare for such possible failures by working on specific coping skills.

Enlisting Client Collaboration

Stress management training should enlist the client and the participants as collaborators in the analysis of the problem and in the development, implementation, and evaluation of the training regimen. Such a collaborative approach reduces the likelihood of client resistance and treatment nonadherence. Moreover, such collaboration encourages clients to adopt a "personal scientist" orientation (Mahoney, 1977) or engage in what Beck, Rush, Hollon, and Shaw (1979) called "collaborative empiricism." Clients can be encouraged and guided to perform "personal experiments" in order to determine the adaptive value of specific coping procedures.

Client Feedback

Stress management training should ensure that the client receives and attends to feedback about the natural consequences of his or her efforts at coping. Such consequences must be viewed as constructive feedback rather than as occasions for "catastrophizing." Moreover, the trainer should encourage clients to make self-attributions about the positive changes that have occurred. Insofar as training can be expanded across trainers, settings, and time, the likelihood of achieving generalization and the durability of the effects increase.

Duration of Training

Consistent with the notion of individually tailoring stress management programs, the duration of the training should be based on the client's performance and not on a predetermined, arbitrarily fixed number of sessions. One should also build follow-up assessments, booster sessions, and follow-through interventions into training whenever feasible. Follow-through interventions refer to the extension of training into subsequent phases such as efforts to teach stress management to job applicants being followed up with subsequent on-the-job stress programs.

Multileveled and Multifaceted Training

Finally, consistent with the transactional model, the intervention and training program should be multileveled and multifaceted. This is *not* a call for an eclectic hodgepodge, but rather a recognition that, given specific analysis of the nature of stress, interventions often need to go beyond the level of participants or the teaching of specific coping skills to clients. In many instances, there is a need to change the social environment, which may inadvertently compound tragedies rather than simply deal with victims.

Table 2.1 summarizes the various guidelines that should be considered in generating and evaluating stress management programs. One can use this checklist as a consumer's guide in evaluating the many training programs and books designed to reduce and avoid stress. Each of these

Table 2.1. Guidelines for Developing Stress Reduction and Prevention Programs

---

 1. Analyze what has to be trained. Intervention may need to be multileveled.
 2. Conduct a careful assessment to determine if intrapersonal and interpersonal factors in-
    hibit implementation of client's coping skills.
 3. Establish a working relationship and enlist client and significant others as collaborators
    in assessment, development, implementation, and evaluation of the training program.
 4. Train a range of coping skills that are sensitive to individual, cultural, and situational
    differences. Foster a flexible coping repertoire.
 5. Be sensitive to the role of cognitive and affective factors in coping.
 6. Select training tasks carefully, making them similar to criterion.
 7. Train for generalization—don't expect it. Training should make the need for and means
    of generalizing explicit.
 8. Ensure that training is future-oriented, anticipating and incorporating possible and real
    failures into the training regimen. Include relapse prevention training.
 9. Train in multiple settings when possible, with multiple trainers on multiple tasks. Have
    the client engage in multiple graded assignments in the clinic (e.g., imagery rehearsal,
    role-playing) and in in vivo graded assignments. Use the notion of graduation or inocula-
    tion as the basis for training.
10. Ensure that the client receives and recognizes feedback about the usefulness of the train-
    ing procedures. Have clients make self-attributions about improvements.
11. Make the length of training dependent on a performance-based criterion, and don't let
    it be time-based (e.g., a fixed number of sessions). Whenever possible, include booster
    sessions, follow-up assessments, and follow-through programs.

---

guidelines is incorporated into the SIT program described in the subsequent chapters.

   While there is much to learn about which coping strategies are most
beneficial for whom and under what conditions, a consideration of the
clinical guidelines offered in this chapter will increase the efficacy of stress
management interventions. The need for such interventions is indicated
by the observation that left to their own devices, people often employ coping mechanisms that exacerbate the very problems that they are designed
to solve (Kessler, Price, & Wortman, 1984). These clinical guidelines might
not only be applicable to professionals who implement stress reduction
procedures, but to informal agents (family, friends, neighbors) who provide most of the support to victims of life crises.

Chapter 3
Stress Inoculation Training: Overview and Applications

SIT[1] is not a single technique. It is a generic term referring to a treatment paradigm consisting of a semistructured, clinically sensitive training regimen. The specific training operations conducted during the course of training vary, depending upon the population treated. SIT combines elements of didactic teaching, Socratic discussion, cognitive restructuring, problem solving and relaxation training, behavioral and imaginal rehearsal, self-monitoring, self-instruction and self-reinforcement, and efforts at environmental change. SIT is designed to nurture and develop coping skills, not only to resolve specific immediate problems but also to apply to future difficulties. It provides individuals and groups with a proactive defense or a set of coping skills to deal with future stressful situations.

In some ways SIT is analogous to the concepts of medical inoculation against biological diseases and attitude-change immunization. Analogous to medical inoculation, SIT is designed to build "psychological antibodies," or coping skills, and to enhance resistance through exposure to stimuli that are strong enough to arouse defenses without being so powerful as to overcome them. In this way, the client can (a) develop a sense of "learned resourcefulness" through experiencing success in coping with manageable levels of stress, and (b) build a prospective defense composed of skills and positive expectations that will help him or her deal effectively with even more stressful situations. More specifically, SIT is designed to:

[1]The history of how Stress Inoculation Training was developed has been described by Meichenbaum (1977) and will not be reiterated here. It is worth noting, however, that the development of SIT was part of a zeitgeist that expressed dissatisfaction with behavior therapy procedures. Interestingly, quite independent of SIT, Marvin Goldfried (1971) at Stony Brook developed a self-control desensitization procedure, and Richard Suinn (1977) at Colorado developed anxiety management training, both having similarities to SIT. SIT is one of several cognitive behavioral treatment procedures that has emerged in the last few years.

1. Teach clients the transactional nature of stress and coping.
2. Train clients to self-monitor maladaptive thoughts, images, feelings, and behaviors in order to facilitate adaptive appraisals.
3. Train clients in problem solving, that is, problem definition, consequence, anticipation, decision making, and feedback evaluation.
4. Model and rehearse direct-action, emotion-regulation, and self-control coping skills.
5. Teach clients how to use maladaptive responses as cues to implement their coping repertoires.
6. Offer practice in in vitro imaginal and in behavioral rehearsal and in vivo graded assignments that become increasingly demanding, to nurture clients' confidence in and utilization of their coping repertoires.
7. Help clients acquire sufficient knowledge, self-understanding, and coping skills to facilitate better ways of handling (un)expected stressful situations.

The SIT regimen has been applied on a treatment and preventative basis to a wide variety of clinical and nonclinical populations, as enumerated in Table 3.1.

SIT has been carried out with individuals, couples, and groups, with the training varying in length from as short as 1 hour with patients about to undergo surgery to 40 one-hour sessions administered to psychiatric patients or to those with chronic clinical problems such as back pain. In most instances, SIT consists of 12 to 15 sessions, plus booster and follow-up sessions faded over a 6-to-12-month period.

Obviously, the way in which the three phases of SIT training (conceptualization, skills acquisition and rehearsal, application and follow-through) are conducted varies, depending upon the length of the training and the nature of the population. The content of the conceptualization phase, the specific skills trained, and the nature of the application phase are geared to the target problems. There is, however, sufficient overlap in the training formats for the various populations for us to consider each of these phases respectively in the next three chapters.

Parenthetically, it should be noted that as SIT has evolved, the three stages have been labeled in several different ways. Initially, they were called *educational*, *rehearsal* and *application* phases. It soon became apparent that this was a misnomer because the entire SIT procedure is educational in nature. Subsequently, the initial stage has been called the *conceptualization phase* since the primary focus of this stage is on establishing a collaborative relationship with clients and on helping them to better understand the nature of stress and its effect on emotion and performance and to reconceptualize it in transactional terms.

The second phase is now called *skills acquisition* and *rehearsal*, during which clients develop and rehearse a variety of coping skills, primarily within the clinic and gradually in vivo. The only reservation about this label is that it should not obscure the possibility that some clients might already have coping skills within their repertoires. However, a variety of intrapersonal and interpersonal factors might inhibit their implementation. Sometimes the task for the trainer is not to teach new coping skills per se but to enlist clients as collaborators in appreciating and removing such inhibitory factors.

The third phase is now called *application and follow-through*, in order to highlight the need for the trainer to consider the important role of booster sessions, follow-up assessments, the need to adopt a future orientation in terms of relapse prevention, and the need to extend training programs into the future. Subsumed under this phase are both in vitro (imaginal and behavioral rehearsal in the clinic) and graded exposure in vivo (performing personal experiments in real life). John Horan and his colleagues, who have conducted nine experiments on SIT in the last 8 years, prefer to call the third phase *exposure training*, limiting it to exposure to in vivo stressors. Our own clinical experience has underscored the need to mix clinical activities (imaginal and behavioral rehearsal) with the feedback one gains from in vivo experience. Thus, we have included both in vitro and in vivo experiences in this third phase.

These distinctions are not merely semantic problems or clinical niceties. They have important implications for various attempts to conduct dismantling studies in order to determine the most important active components in SIT. For example, several studies have found that the educational stage (now called *conceptualization phase*) without a coping skills stage (skills acquisition and rehearsal phase) was no different from a no-treatment or placebo treatment group, and one cannot readily conduct the skills training without the initial conceptualization phase (West, Horan, & Games, 1984). There is now a need for SIT researchers to agree on similar nomenclature for the various phases, and the present labels of *conceptualization*, *skills acquisition* and *rehearsal*, *application* and *follow-through* are proposed as the best labels to capture the current sense of the procedure.

Also of interest is the fact that SIT training has been conducted by a variety of different trainers. Although most of the studies cited in Table 3.1 were led by a trained mental health professional (e.g., psychologist or mental health counselor), a number of investigators have trained others to conduct SIT (e.g., probation officers with adolescent offenders, police officers with other police, military drill instructors with other instructors, nurses with patients, and teachers with students). We will comment further on the use of such individuals in SIT training in chapter 7. For now it is important to appreciate that one of the strengths of SIT is its flexibility and its "portability"—application by various levels of professionals and "paraprofessionals." Such portability should not hide the fact that clinical

Table 3.1. Application of Stress Inoculation Training and
Closely-Related Stress Management Procedures

TARGET POPULATION	REFERENCES
Problems with anger	
Adults with anger-control problems	Bistline & Frieden, 1984; Gaertner, Craighead, & Horan, 1983; Novaco, 1975, 1977a
Adolescents with anger-control problems	Feindler & Fremouw, 1983; Feindler, Marriott, & Iwata, 1984; Schlichter & Horan, 1981
Abusive parents	Denicola & Sandler, 1980; Egan, 1983
Problems with anxiety	
Test anxiety	Deffenbacher & Hahloser, 1981; Hussain & Lawrence, 1978; Meichenbaum, 1972; Nye, 1979
Interpersonal and dating anxiety	Glass, Gottman, & Shmurak, 1976; Jaremko, 1983
Public speaking anxiety	Craddock, Cotler, & Jason, 1978; Fremouw & Zitter, 1978; Jaremko, 1980; Jaremko, Hadfield, & Walker, 1980; Kantor, 1978
Performance anxiety (e.g., musical, writing)	Altmaier, Ross, Leary, & Thornbrough, 1982; Kendrick, 1979; Salovey & Harr, 1983; Sweeney & Horan, 1982
Anxiety over transition to high school	Jason & Burrows, 1983
Anxiety of adults reentering university	Athabasca University, 1983
Problems with circumscribed fears	
Multiple animal phobias	Meichenbaum & Cameron, 1972
Fear of flying	Girodo & Roehl, 1978
Prevention of fears in children and adults	Barrios & Shigetomi, 1980; Poser & King, 1975, 1976
General stress reactions	
Community residents who experience stress	Long, 1982, 1984, in press a
Clients in community mental health center	Brown, 1980
"Neurotic" patients in acute treatment facility	Holcomb, 1979
Medical outpatients	Cragan & Deffenbacher, 1984
Women on public assistance	Tableman, Marciniak, Johnson, & Rodgers, 1982
Type A individuals	Jenni & Wollersheim, 1979; Roskies, 1983; Suinn, 1982; Thurman, 1984
Medical problems—Prevention	
Prepare cardiac patients for open heart surgery	Erdahl & Blythe, 1984
Prepare adult patients for cardiac catherization procedures	Kendall, 1983; Kendall, Williams, Pechacek, Graham, Sisslak, & Herzoff, 1979
Prepare adult patients for surgery	Langer, Janis, & Wolfer, 1975
Prepare children for dental examinations and surgery	Melamed, 1982; Melamed & Siegel, 1975; Siegel & Peterson, 1980

Table 3.1 (*continued*)

TARGET POPULATION	REFERENCES
Health-related problems	
General pain patients	Levendusky & Pankrantz, 1975; Rybstein-Blinchik, 1979; Turk, Meichenbaum, & Genest, 1983
Cancer patients (adults and children)	Moore & Altmaier, 1981; Varni, Jay, Masek, & Thompson, in press; Weisman, Worden, & Sobel, 1980
Rheumatoid arthritics	Randich, 1982
Patients with chronic tension headaches	Holroyd & Andrasik, 1978; Holroyd, Andrasik, & Westbrook, 1977
Burn patients	Wernick, 1983; Wernick, Jaremko, & Taylor, 1981
Essential hypertensive patients	Jorgensen, Houston, & Zurawski, 1981
Patients experiencing dysmenorrhea	Quillen & Denney, 1982
Dental fear and pain	Klepac, Hague, Dowling, & McDonald, 1981
Lab analogue pain and stress studies	
Cold pressor test	Girodo & Wood, 1979; Hackett & Horan, 1980; Hackett, Horan, Buchanan, & Zumoff, 1979; Horan, Hackett, Buchanan, Stone, & Demchik-Stone, 1977; Vallis, 1984; Worthington, 1978; Worthington & Shumate, 1981
Muscle ischemia test	Genest, 1979; Turk, 1977
Arm shock pain	Klepac, Hague, Dowling, & McDonald, 1981
Ego threatening interpersonal encounters	Ulissi, 1978
Stress-engendering film clips	Ulissi, 1978
Victim populations	
Rape victims	Veronen & Kilpatrick, 1983
Victims of terrorist attacks	Ayalon, 1983
Professional groups	
Registered nurses	West, Horan, & Games, 1984
Practical nursing students	Wernick, 1984
School psychologists	Forman, 1981
Teachers	Forman, 1982; Turk, Meeks, & Turk, 1982
Police officers	Novaco, 1977b; Sarason, Johnson, Berberich, & Siegel, 1979
Probation officers	Novaco, 1980
Military recruit trainees	Novaco, Cook, & Sarason, 1983
Parachutists	Dinner & Gal, 1983
Marine Corps drill instructors	Novaco, Cook, & Sarason, 1983
Scuba divers	Deikis, 1982
Athletes stress management	Kirschenbaum, Wittrock, Smith, & Monson, 1984; Long, 1980; Smith, 1980

skills are needed in conducting SIT training. This is particularly important when we appreciate that the goals of training are likely to change over
time. For example, in the SIT training of pain patients, the initial treatment objective might be symptom relief, but, with improvement, the treatment goals for both the patient and family members can shift to issues
of vocational readjustment, marital conflict, and the like. As these shifts
occur, there is a need to recycle the three phases. It is important to recognize that the three phases do not represent a lockstep progression. They
are often marked by overlap and interdependence. The SIT trainer does
not attempt to stick rigidly to any one technique but selects from the range
of techniques the one that seems most appropriate at the time.

Although the next three chapters suggest a linear progression through
the various phases, in practice the phases blend together. For instance,
although assessment is the main focus of the first phase, reassessment
is an ongoing process throughout the other two phases. In fact, in SIT,
assessment and treatment are inseparable, as there is a continual reassessment and revision of goals. Similarly, the other phases might also be
recycled.

The multifaceted features of SIT are illustrated by the many references
listed in Table 3.1. Space does not permit a detailed evaluation of these
studies. The interested reader should see Meichenbaum and Jaremko
(1983), Turk et al. (1983), or the other cited references. At this stage in the
development of SIT, one can conclude that the outcome of research on
SIT is encouraging and improving. It remains necessary, however, to
observe that many of the studies cited in Table 3.1 are "demonstration"
projects often lacking in important methodological checks. The methodological limitations include the absence of long-term follow-up assessments, the absence of multiple measures, the absence of manipulation and
credibility checks for SIT and the comparison control groups, the absence
of checks for demand characteristics, and, in some studies, confounds
with prior exposure to stressors. It is to be hoped that future research will
overcome these methodological limitations, providing much-needed evaluations of SIT. To nurture such evaluations, the next three chapters consider SIT in some detail.

Finally, it is important to appreciate that SIT can be combined with other
interventions. For example, in the work with chronic pain patients described by Turk et al. (1983), SIT was part of an overall therapy regimen
that included medical treatments, physiotherapy, vocational counseling,
and patient self-help groups. SIT is designed to supplement and enhance
the clinician's tools.

Chapter 4
Conceptualization Phase

The initial conceptualization phase of SIT constitutes approximately one-sixth to one-third of the training. This applies whether the training constitutes 1 hour of preparation with surgical patients or 20 sessions with pain patients. The objectives of this phase are to:

1. Establish a collaborative relationship with the client and with significant others where appropriate (e.g., spouse),
2. Discuss the client's stress-related problems and symptoms, focusing on a situational analysis,
3. Collect information in the form of interviews, questionnaires, self-monitoring procedures, imagery-based techniques, and behavioral assessments,
4. Assess the client's expectations with regard to effectiveness of the training program and formulate treatment plans, establishing short, intermediate, and long-term goals,
5. Educate the client about the transactional nature of stress and coping and consider the role that cognitions and emotions play in engendering and maintaining stress,
6. Offer a conceptual model or reconceptualization of the client's stress reactions,
7. Anticipate and subsume possible client resistance and reasons for treatment nonadherence.

Before we consider the specific steps to achieve these goals, there is a need to comment briefly on the important role of the client-trainer relationship and the nature of the trainer's style.

RELATIONSHIP FACTORS IN SIT

Most stress management programs emphasize the variety of specific interventions that clients are taught. These programs usually do not emphasize the important role of the client-trainer relationship, which provides the framework in which coping skills are nurtured. Waterhouse and

Strupp (1984) have recently underscored the role of the therapeutic relationship in mediating behavior change. As they described it, the trainer's ability to build rapport, to convey a sense of "I am in this with you," to establish a collaborative working relationship, all facilitated change. Interestingly, the quality of the client-trainer relationship established early in therapy (by the third session) proved an important predictor of outcome. Insofar as clients felt accepted, understood, and liked by the trainer, treatment tended to be successful. If the client's viewpoint is not adequately addressed, then client satisfaction and adherence can be jeopardized.

The trainer's or therapist's style, as well as client characteristics, plays an important role in establishing an atmosphere where clients feel comfortable to self-disclose their thoughts and feelings. Warmth, a desire to accurately understand, cooperative intentions, and conveying a sense of genuine acceptance and optimism, all engender a trusting relationship. For example, Rodin (1979) suggested that, when a client mentions something unfavorable, the trainer can respond with a statement such as "It's understandable that you would feel self-critical at times and want to change." When something favorable is mentioned, the trainer could react: "It is clear that you have a lot going for you." Such statements are designed to convey a sense of worth that will help to mobilize a desire to change. If a client believes that his or her opinion is valued and worthwhile, then the client will develop a sense of efficacy and convey expectations and beliefs about treatment.

As Dunbar (1980) noted, such characteristics as the trainer's "hurriedness, interruptions, lack of time for listening, inattentiveness, and not identifying the patient's problems from the patient's own perspective will interfere with the therapist's approachability" (p. 80). An awareness of these characteristics is especially important when one is working with clients who have recently experienced major stressful life events such as the unexpected death of a loved one or other personal disaster or with clients who suffer from posttraumatic stress disorder. In such instances, it is important to establish a safe relationship and create a comfortable climate where the trainer or therapist takes the time to listen to an unrushed recounting of the client's stressful events (e.g., personal disaster or crisis). The trainer can use his or her "humaness" by genuinely conveying how he or she is moved by the client's experience, reflecting on how frightening and upsetting the stressful event must have been.

On the one hand, the trainer should facilitate the client's gradual self-disclosure of such affect-laden material, but, on the other hand, the trainer should encourage the client *not* to reveal that which he or she feels unready to reveal or is uncomfortable about. The client must feel secure that the self-disclosure of such material is under his or her own control. The trainer's nondemanding presence should convey to the client permission to "dose" one's feelings rather than the necessity to work through or feel overwhelmed by the affect-related material associated with stressful events. In this way the client can recount at his or her own pace stressful experiences, sharing any intense recurrent intrusive feelings, images, and thoughts (e.g., "I keep asking myself if I did enough" "Why not me?" "I keep seeing her face"). The trainer can begin the reconceptualization process in response to such outpourings by conveying the universality of such stress responses. It is important for stressed clients to recognize that such emotional distress is not a sign of maladjustment or a sign that one is "going crazy," but that others who endured the same stressful events have had similar feelings and experiences. Stress should be viewed as a normal course of such life experiences. When SIT is conducted on a group basis, such mutual self-disclosure can contribute to the "normalization" process. (See Cohen and Ahearn, 1980, for a more detailed account of how disaster victims can be counseled.)

Often, stressed clients enter training with an internal dialogue of helplessness and hopelessness, feelings of being demoralized, and a "paralysis of will." They also often have concerns about what Raimy (1975) called "phrenophobia," a fear of going crazy. An important feature of the initial phase of SIT is to begin to change the client's internal dialogue about his or her stress reactions. The trainer's style plays an important role in conveying reassurance and in helping clients refocus attention on the present and future rather than dwelling on events in the past.

By establishing a collaborative relationship, the trainer can help clients redevelop a sense of control and refocus on personal resources, prior life accomplishments, and prior positive achievements. The mutual formulation by both client and trainer of the nature of the problem and the establishment of a treatment plan can help nurture such a collaborative relationship. By offering his or her ideas tentatively while soliciting candid reactions from clients, the trainer can create an ambiance that encourages free exchange of information, including client expressions of misunderstandings or misgivings. The trainer is more Socratic than didactic. In fact, the trainer might wish to emulate that fine clinician . . . the television detective character, Columbo, as portrayed by the actor Peter Falk. As you may recall, Columbo used his own befuddlement and bemusement as a means of soliciting information and as a means of having others try on a particular perspective or conceptualization. For example, the trainer might ask:

> I am not sure if I quite understood, can we go over that one more time?
>
> I am wondering in what ways your becoming stressed in situation . . . is like your becoming stressed in situation. . . ?
>
> On the one hand I hear you saying . . . and on the other hand I hear you saying . . . I wonder how these two things go together.
>
> Correct me if I am wrong, but what I hear you saying is?

SIT-B*

You seem to be telling me . . . Am I correct in assuming that . . . ?

I get the feeling that . . . , Is that the way you see it?

We have covered a lot of territory so far, is there anything I said that troubled you?[1]

Such probes are designed to engender a collaborative, empathic, genuine search by both client and trainer to better understand what is going on when the client is stressed, what internal and external events trigger stressful reactions, and moreover, what can be done to change the situation. The trainer tries to view the world through the client's eyes, tapping any particular current concerns or private fears a client might have. For example, with pain patients, the SIT trainer stated:

> Many people we see have private fears about what's wrong with them. In the back of their minds, they have concerns that they have been hesitant to express to others, or sometimes even to themselves. Have you had such feelings and thoughts?

Moreover, the trainer might try to anticipate and subsume a client's particular concerns by raising them rather than letting them remain covert. Some clients feel intimidated about raising concerns, and the trainer can facilitate such discussion. For example, the therapist might state: "A question that has often been raised by other clients is _____, and although this may not have crossed your mind or been a concern, let us consider it for a moment." A number of issues can be raised in this manner.

The point to be underscored is that, although the SIT approach is relatively structured and action-oriented, the trainer needs to be a sensitive, caring, thoughtful clinician. The trainer is not delivering a series of lectures on stress and coping nor is he or she strictly imposing a rigidly established curriculum. Rather, the trainer is constantly interacting with and enlisting the client's collaboration and individually tailoring the assessments and interventions. The object of SIT is not to remove or eliminate stress but to encourage clients to view stressful situations as problems-to-be-solved rather than as personal threats. The goal is to make clients better problem solvers to deal with future stressful events as they might arise.

It is important to note that not only must the client learn anticipatory problem-solving skills but so must the trainer, in order to avoid possible sources of client resistance and treatment nonadherence. The following example will illustrate the ways in which the trainer can engage in such

---

[1]Although detailed scripts are provided, the procedures *should not* be implemented in a mechanical, rote fashion. One must learn and practice how to customize treatment techniques to the specific needs, beliefs, and circumstances of the client. Clinical dexterity is the byword for the training.

problem-solving activity. For instance, one potential source of client re-sistance might derive from referral and intake processes. If a medical pa-tient is referred for SIT after physical tests have been completed and have proven negative, the patient could infer that the referral implies that his or her problem is being dismissed as "imaginary." Such an interpreta-tion might result in the client's resisting the establishment of a working relationship with the trainer. To avoid such potential problems, the trainer needs to encourage and coach referral sources on when and how to refer and to prepare clients for SIT.

In short, the trainer must be very sensitive to what his or her clients are told about the nature of the training prior to entry. Turk et al. (1983) have discussed how trainers should work with referral agents on an ongoing basis to provide both descriptions of SIT and feedback about outcome. The transactional model not only applies to the client's treatment, but it is also a pervasive mode embracing the entire training regimen.[2] From this vantage point the SIT trainer is viewed as a creative problem solver and *not* a technician implementing a treatment protocol.

DATA COLLECTION AND INTEGRATION

The initial task for the trainer is to establish a relationship with the client and to solicit information that will help in the formulation of a training plan that can be individually tailored to the specific client's needs and strengths. During this initial assessment phase it is important to keep in mind that the types of questions the trainer asks, the assessment instru-ments employed, and the therapy rationale offered are all seen as actively contributing to the training process. In turn, we will consider the clinical interview, imagery-based assessment, self-monitoring, behavioral assess-ments, and standardized tests and questionnaires as means of assessment and client involvement.

Interview

SIT usually begins with a semistructured interview that is tailored to the specific population. Obviously, the way in which one structures the interview with a postdisaster client versus a Type A businessman who does not see that he has a stress-related problem would differ; or a medical

[2]Even the ambiance of the setting has proven important to outcome, as noted by the finding that the length of time clients spend in the waiting room correlates with treatment nonadherence (Davidson, 1976; Dunbar, 1980). The client may feel the trainer is uninterested or too busy and that his or her problems are too trivial to warrant attention. Such findings underscore the need for SIT trainers to be sen-sitive to their own styles and the context in which the training is offered.

patient whose pain is stress-related, as in the case of someone suffering from headaches, versus someone who works in a stress-related occupation. Although differences would appear across these various interviews, the common factor would be the interviewer's style of inquiry and the common search to identify developmental and current determinants of the client's stressful reactions.

In terms of style, the interview is conducted in a gentle, probing fashion, for much of the needed information will likely emerge as clients relate their tales and discuss their stress reactions. The interview is not a cross-examination but an organized systematic attempt to better understand the client's stress and coping experiences.

More specifically, the interview process, which might occur over several sessions, is designed to:

1. Elicit examples of stressful events and reactions and increase clients' awareness of their contribution to the stress reaction;
2. Assess clients' expectations about training;
3. Provide a cognitive-functional analysis of the internal and external determinants of stressful reactions so that clients can become aware of low-intensity cues that signal the onset of stressful reactions;
4. Examine, in a collaborative manner, the communalities or themes that occur across stressful situations;
5. Consider with clients the impact stress has on daily functioning; and
6. Collaboratively formulate treatment goals and training plans.

A number of structured interviews (e.g., see Table 4.1) have been offered to solicit such information. (Note that in the Peterson interview in Table 4.1 the word *problem* could readily be replaced with the word *stress reactions*.) Related questions that cover the topic of stress are offered in Table 4.2.

As the client describes stressful situations, it is important to encourage detailed accounts. One would like to know what aspects of the stressful situation(s) the client attends to, what thoughts pass through his or her mind, what is experienced emotionally, what behaviors are produced, and how significant others respond.

Imagery-based Recall

A useful means of helping a client report such information is to use an imagery-based recall procedure. Such imagery recall is often useful in helping a client attend to aspects and details of his or her stress response that might otherwise have been overlooked or underemphasized in a direct interview. In this way, the client can share as part of the transactional process thoughts, images, feelings, and behaviors that could have

Table 4.1. The Clinical Interview

I. Definition of problem behavior
   A. Nature of the problem as defined by client
      "As I understand it, you came here because . . . " (Discuss reasons for contact as stated by referral agency or other source of information.) "I would like you to tell me more about this. What is the problem as you see it?" (Probe as needed to determine client's view of the problem behavior, i.e., what he or she is doing, or failing to do, that the client or somebody else defines as a problem.)
   B. Severity of the problem
      1. "How serious a problem is this as far as you are concerned?" (Probe to determine client's view of the problem behavior, i.e., what he or she is doing, or failing to do, or that somebody else defines as a problem.)
      2. "How often do you (exhibit problem behavior, if a disorder of commission, or have occasion to exhibit desired behavior, if a problem of omission)?" (The goal is to obtain information regarding frequency of response.)
   C. Generality of the problem
      1. Duration
         "How long has this been going on?"
      2. Extent
         "Where does the problem usually come up?" (Probe to determine situations in which problem behavior occurs, e.g., "Do you feel that way at work? How about at home?")
II. Determinants of problem behavior
   A. Conditions that intensify problem behavior
      "Now I want you to think about the times when (the problem) is worst. What sorts of things are going on then?"
   B. Conditions that alleviate problem behavior
      "What about the times when (the problem) gets better? What sorts of things are going on then?"
   C. Perceived origins
      "What do you think is causing (the problem)?"
   D. Specific antecedents
      "Think back to the last time (the problem) occurred. What was going on at that time?"
      As needed:
      1. Social influences
         "Were any other people around? Who? What were they doing?"
      2. Personal influences
         "What were you thinking about at the time? How did you feel?"
   E. Specific consequences
      "What happened after (the problem occurred)?"
      As needed:
      1. Social consequences
         "What did (significant others identified above) do?"
      2. Personal consequences
         "How did that make you feel?"
   F. Suggested changes
      "You have thought a lot about (the problem). What do you think might be done to improve the situation?"
   G. Suggested leads for further inquiry
      "What else do you think I should find out about to help you with this problem?"

Note. From *The Clinical Study of Social Behavior* by Donald R. Peterson, (1968), Englewood Cliffs, NJ: Prentice-Hall, pp. 121–122. Copyright 1968 by Prentice-Hall, Inc. Reprinted by permission.

Table 4.2. Clinical Interview Focusing on Questions About Stress

---

Have you felt stressed recently?

What specific problems have you been grappling with? On what basis do you say that?

How do you know when you are stressed? What are some of the things you do, feel, and think? What kinds of bodily signs or symptoms do you use to tell how stressed you are?

How long have you had such reactions?

What sort of things (events) do you find most stressful?

How do such reactions affect you? How do these reactions interfere with your life? Do they prevent you from doing some things you would want to do?

Under what specific circumstances do these stressful reactions occur?

What sorts of things seem to make the stress worse? Better?

What would you be doing differently if your stressful reactions were controlled or removed?

How would life be different if your stressful reactions could be relieved?

What sorts of things have you tried to alleviate your stress? How have they worked?

Given all that happens to you, how can you best take care of yourself?

What do you expect will happen here in our sessions?

What would you like to have happen?

What would it take to change?

On what will the outcome of the training depend?

---

contributed to his or her stress. The goal is to help the client appreciate that one is not merely a victim of stress. Instead, how one appraises events—how one feels, thinks, and behaves—can contribute to one's stress level. The initial interviews and imagery-recall procedure are designed to enlist the client as collaborator in collecting data whereby he or she comes to entertain a transactional perspective.

More specifically, the trainer, following the initial probes, can ask the client to do something a bit unusual, namely, to sit back in the chair, close his or her eyes, and imagine or relive in the mind's eye one or several recent experiences of stress. The client should recall the experience as clearly as possible and visualize it as if he or she were there at the moment.

Just settle back in the chair, close your eyes, and think about the experience. Take your time, there's no rush. Just replay the stressful event in your imagination as if you were rerunning a movie in slow motion. Begin at the point just before you felt distressed. For example, Don, when you were going to put your four children to bed. Perhaps, you can begin at the point when you are starting to drive home from work. Just go through the whole experience and see what comes to mind. Describe anything you remember noticing, thinking, feeling, or doing.

Once the trainer has solicited the client's thoughts and feelings surrounding significant events, the trainer can ask the client what if any impact such thoughts and feelings had on his or her stress level. Then the trainer asks if there have been similar thoughts and feelings in other situations. In this way the trainer can conduct a situational analysis to determine if particular themes or current concerns are evident across stressful situations. The trainer uses his or her "Columbo routine" of juxtaposing data in exploring the possibility of such themes.

In searching for these common themes or current concerns, (e.g., issues of control or concerns about fairness or social approval), the trainer uses specific examples of the client's thoughts and feelings. For example, if we go back to the incident of my putting my children to bed, the trainer can ask if the specific thoughts and feelings I experienced about being over-whelmed, about fairness and control, occur in other situations in which I become stressed. Such a question should not be asked in an abstract manner, but, instead, the trainer should use the client's own words and pictures, thoughts and feelings, in querying the client about whether he or she has similar reactions in other situations.

> The feelings and thoughts you have such as, "Oh no, not again. Damn it, how many times have I told them. I don't believe she's going out again. The chaos gets too much. All I wanted to do was watch one crummy program"— do you have similar reactions in other situations?

In this way, the trainer can then juxtapose the various events (e.g., becoming upset with putting kids to bed, when the computer goes down, when graduate students don't fulfill assignments, or when a certain relative arrives unexpectedly.) The trainer, using his or her Columbo routine of befuddlement, searches with the client for what is common across these various situations. Note that, by asking the client how such events are alike, the trainer is implying some common thread. Often it is enough to ask about such comparisons and not secure an answer, merely framing the question and planting a seed for future sessions. The trainer might note that such comparisons are something the client may wish to think about and examine in future sessions. In subsequent sessions the client will be asked to self-monitor various stressful events, and these can also be juxtaposed as one attempts to search for commonalities. Such juxta-position of data need not occur in the first session but might be better delayed to subsequent sessions when enough incidents have been raised.

An interesting means of exploring the nature of clients' current concerns has been offered by Goldfried and Goldfried (1980). They described a way of tapping the connotative meaning assigned to events or objects. Clients are given an associative task of completing such sentences as "If this other person disagreed with me, it would upset me because . . . " or "Mak-ing a mistake in front of other people would upset me because. . . ." Such probes aid clients in recognizing and subsequently reevaluating the im-plicit meanings they assign to situations in their lives.

Before we examine other assessment procedures, let us consider the image-recall procedure in a bit more detail, because it provides a useful avenue for considering a number of clinical guidelines. Imagine asking clients to sit back in their chairs, to close their eyes and replay in their mind's eye a stressful incident, sharing the thoughts and feelings that preceded, accompanied and followed the incident. For the sake of argument, let us assume that a client says:

> I didn't have any thoughts and feelings when I put the kids to bed. They are just a bunch of disobedient children.

In short, the imagery-recall procedure *did not work* in soliciting information needed to generate a transactional perspective of stress. What are the different things you might say to yourself at this point? One possibility is:

> I knew Meichenbaum and SIT were full of baloney (or worse). Who needs all this cognitive stuff? Just teach coping skills.

Let me suggest several alternatives, because one of my goals is to influence your internal dialogue the next time you see a client or conduct a workshop. For me, conducting psychotherapy and SIT is hard work, because I spend a fair amount of time "talking to myself," monitoring not only the client's behavior but also my own. I am operating like a decision tree, wondering why the particular procedure did not work.

First, it is possible that the client did *not* in fact have such thoughts. Should one accept the client's statement at face value, suspecting that the stressful reaction played itself out in an automatic "mindless" or scripted fashion, à la Abelson, 1976 and Langer, 1975? If indeed this is the case, it might still be possible for the client to collect data about cognitive and affective events and processes in the future in the form of self-monitoring. Moreover, the failure of attempts to solicit automatic thoughts and feelings does not preclude the use of subsequent aspects of the SIT training that will be described in the next two chapters.

Second, it is possible that the absence of such a self-report during the image recall could be due to a number of other reasons, for example,

1. Clients might have thoughts and feelings that accompany stressful events, but they might be reluctant to self-disclose this material,
2. Clients might not understand the nature of the request (that is, such imagery exercises could be "strange"),
3. Clients might not be sufficiently "psychologically minded" or verbally facile to express such feelings.

The task for the trainer is to conduct an analysis of the reasons why the imagery-recall procedure "did not work." One obvious way to proceed is to ask the client about his or her experience during the image-recall exercise and to tailor the procedure accordingly. A related approach is for the trainer to anticipate such potential difficulties and to include them in the SIT regimen from the outset.

For example, the trainer can use the clinical ploy of an "imaginary other client" to anticipate and to subsume possible client concerns about self-disclosing in training. Some clients may be concerned about who the trainer or therapist "represents."

> If I share my real thoughts about the kids would you tell the police, the doc-tors? Could I lose the kids? What kind of parent would have such thoughts and feelings? What would the trainer (and others) think of me?

> If I told you how upset and depressed I am, would I be sent to the hospital or given shock treatment?

Such reactions can interfere with self-disclosure not only in the imagery-recall procedure but also in the interview. The trainer should spell out at the outset the terms of treatment dealing with issues of confidentiality and trust. Moreover, the trainer can also pull out of his or her back pocket another imaginery client or clients who could voice similar concerns. For example, the trainer might say to the client:

> I'm not sure if this is an issue for you, but on other occasions, clients like yourself have expressed some concern about what they could talk about in training. Was it all right to really share the true feelings they had when they became stressed? . . . I am not sure if you have similar concerns.

Quite often the use of an imaginary other client acts as a catalyst for disinhibiting clients' reactions. We will consider further on how the trainer can judiciously use the imaginary-other procedure as a means of antici-pating and subsuming possible client resistance and treatment nonad-herence, as in the case of self-monitoring.

In the same way that the trainer can anticipate the client's concerns about self-disclosure, the trainer can also anticipate difficulties the client might have in comprehending or performing the imagery-recall task. One way to convey to clients what is requested is for the trainer to model such self-disclosure in the form of examples from his or her (or others') life ex-perience. For example, in working with abusive parents, the trainer could disclose the trials and tribulations, the nature of one's reactions when handling one's own children. The trainer might share a brief anecdote (similar to the one offered at the beginning of this book about the bed-time scenario). Such examples convey that the trainer, who is usually viewed by clients as a competent mastery model, can also have similar stressful experiences with accompanying stress-engendering cognitive and affective reactions. The chosen anecdote should illustrate the transactional nature of stress and convey a coping (not a mastery) model.

Such self-disclosure by either the trainer or other clients when the SIT training is conducted on a group basis acts to "normalize" clients' reactions, as they come to appreciate that they are not alone in having certain types of thoughts and feelings. This identification process is enhanced if groups are composed of individuals who are experiencing similar stressful demands (e.g., widows, police officers).

The trainer's self-disclosure should be supplemented with both an explanation of the rationale underlying the imagery-recall procedure and specific instructions that invite relaxed reflection and detailed responding. For example, the trainer might state:

> In order for us both to better understand why you became so stressed when putting the children to bed, I would like you to reexamine the incident in more detail, reconsidering what exactly happened. Consider what you did and what, if any, thoughts and feelings you experienced before, during, and after the incident. In this way, we can become aware of the chain of events of your reactions and what the children did and perhaps figure out how the situation got out of hand. In this way, we will both be able to get in tune with what it is that seems to "trigger your fuse" (i.e., low-intensity cues).

Some clients probably require the trainer's assistance in conducting the imagery-recall exercise to identify specifics and details of the situation such as encouraging the client to notice colors, sounds, smells. The trainer can ask clients about the scenes they visualize and then discuss the impact of such thoughts and feelings on their stress reactions. Such post hoc data analysis can be supplemented with information obtained from self-monitoring.

In summary, when the trainer tries one of the proposed SIT procedures and it does not work or achieve the training objectives, then the occasion arises for the trainer to talk to himself or herself in ways that analyze the variety of different reasons for possible failure. Client and trainer work together in a collaborative fashion to collect relevant information, as in self-monitoring.

Self-monitoring

A major feature of SIT is having clients become collaborators or "personal scientists" by means of self-monitoring. A variety of different forms of self-monitoring have been used in SIT, each tailored to the characteristics of a specific population. Self-monitoring has ranged from clients' keeping an open-ended diary to their systematically recording or rating specific thoughts, feelings, and behaviors. Such behaviors as daily hassles, stress logs, parental stress episodes, anger incidents, pain intensity ratings, drug intake, depressogenic thoughts, and the like have been covered. Often, different self-monitoring procedures are used in combination: for example, an open-ended diary followed by more specific assessment procedures. Because the different self-monitoring procedures have been described elsewhere (Nelson, 1977; Turk et al., 1983), the present discussion focuses on clinical guidelines for using self-monitoring procedures. All too often, treatment manuals focus on the specific features of a clinical procedure such as self-monitoring and relaxation without discussing how one prepares, instructs, or uses the procedure. Nor do manuals amply consider the potential ways of handling client resistance and treatment nonadherence.

Solicit Client Suggestion. The first clinical guideline should be viewed as a general strategy to be employed in all stages of SIT. It is proposed that the training is most successful when the trainer can have the client suggest the specific procedure that is to be undertaken. Rather than have the trainer introduce a specific procedure such as self-monitoring, the trainer is at his or her "therapeutic best" when the client is just one step ahead of the trainer in suggesting specific procedures. In this way, the client views the suggestion for the need to self-monitor, practice relaxation, engage in personal experiments, and so forth as his or her own. In order to accomplish this objective, the trainer needs to lay the groundwork by means of the questions asked, the reflections offered, and the rationale and examples given.

The trainer lays the groundwork for self-monitoring by conducting a clinical interview detailing a situational and cognitive-affective analysis of the client's stress reactions. Having taken a phenomenological perspective of the client's stress, the trainer can then state:

> We have spent some very useful time discussing the nature of your stress and its impact on you and others. I am wondering how we might be able to understand in even more detail exactly when you become distressed, what triggers your stress reactions and what exactly goes on? . . . I am wondering how we might get a better handle on the nature of the stress that you experience on a daily basis, say between now and our next session?

It is not a big jump for clients to suggest that it might prove helpful if they could just keep track of when they feel stressed.

> Keep track of your stress, that sounds like a good idea. Do you have any thoughts about how you might, in fact, do that?

The trainer then solicits the client's suggestions and discusses his or her previous experience with keeping diaries and self-monitoring (noticing or observing his or her ongoing behavior). The trainer can also build upon the client's suggestions by using the imaginary other client.

> It is interesting that you mention keeping track of your stress, because we have found that with other clients like yourself who have experienced similar

stress reactions, they too have found it useful to systematically record information about their stress reactions. Such information has helped them appreciate how their stress often varies across situations and over time and exactly what factors influence their stress reactions. . . . In many ways, the
clients enjoyed the task of becoming their own Sherlock Holmes in figuring
out the nature of their stress.

In short, it is felt that clients demonstrate greater interest and treatment
adherence if they feel they are contributing and if they see the value of
each of the steps in the training.

Make Simple Requests. Laying the groundwork as well as soliciting the
client's suggestions about the specific procedure of self-monitoring is only
the first step. This is followed by a straightforward and simple description
of what is required and why. The simpler the request, the greater the likelihood of compliance. For example, hourly self-monitoring is less likely
to be followed than intermediate recording (once per morning, afternoon,
and evening).

> Because each client's problem is different, and because it is important for
> both of us to understand your stress reaction (pain, anger, etc.) in as much
> detail as possible so we can choose the best treatment program, I would like
> you to keep a daily diary of your stress. Have you ever kept a diary be-
> fore? . . . Well, the diary I am going to ask you to keep is quite simple. It in-
> volves answering a few questions about your stress each day. It does not take
> much time. Other clients like yourself have indicated that such daily infor-
> mation has proven quite revealing and helpful. Let me explain exactly what
> is involved.

The trainer then describes the process by which the client is to learn to
listen with a "third ear," noticing when he or she is stressed. Such
recognition is to serve as a cue for the client to pause for a few seconds
in order to try to identify the situation, the feelings, and the accompanying thoughts that pass through his or her mind.

Obtain a Comprehension Check. Following the explanation of a specific self-
monitoring procedure, there is a need to obtain a comprehension check
to ensure that the client has indeed understood what it is that is being
asked and why. The client is asked to restate the assignment and the
reasons for it in his or her own words. As DiMatteo and DiNicola (1982)
noted, quite often huge communication gaps exist between a trainer or
a therapist and the average client. Care must be taken that all information is phrased in nontechnical, unambiguous terms. The necessary information may be repeated on several occasions, and checks for the client's
comprehension should be conducted. One way that SIT trainers have
assessed the client's understanding has been to use a role-reversal pro-

cedure whereby the client is asked to play the role of the trainer, and the trainer plays the role of a new client. For example, the trainer says:

We have covered quite a bit of material in terms of your keeping track of your distress (pain, anger, depression, whatever applies in the individual instance). In order to ensure that you have a clear understanding of what it is you have agreed to do, I am wondering if we could review it for a moment. One way we have found useful is to ask you to imagine for the moment that I am another client like yourself and that you are going to explain in your own words what it is you are going to do to keep track of your daily stress and also why you are going to undertake this effort. How will keeping track of your stress help?

Such a role-reversal process can be a useful supplement to discussion of the client's thoughts and feelings about undertaking the self-monitoring exercise. Such efforts are important in helping to clarify any misunderstanding. The trainer should provide the client with enough time to voice objectives.

Forestall Client Noncompliance. The task of asking clients to self-monitor is yet incomplete. The trainer must consider with the client possible factors that might interfere with compliance with the self-monitoring. The trainer needs to anticipate and subsume all of the possible reasons why the client might not conduct the self-monitoring task. The trainer might state:

I can see that you have a real understanding of what it is you are to do to keep track of your stress and the reasons why doing so would be of help. There is, however, one other question I have. I am wondering what problems, if any, you foresee in carrying out the task you set yourself of conscientiously keeping track of your stress reactions?

The client is given an opportunity to plan ahead for possible difficulties, lapses, or slips. Some clients convey assurances that they will have no problems. The trainer's rejoinder is to encourage and praise such enthusiasm and also to be the pragmatist. The trainer notes,

I can appreciate your keenness in wanting to get on with the task, but I am reminded of clients very much like yourself and some of the difficulties they experienced. I recall seeing one client in the waiting room busily filling out his self-monitoring form for several days. Although he was supposed to record his stress reactions (e.g., anger episodes) as soon as possible after they occurred, somehow he had forgotten, and he was now trying to make up for this by filling out several days in the waiting room. Do you think such problems in remembering to record might occur in your case?

At this point, the trainer solicits the client's reactions and discusses various strategies that could be employed to anticipate memory lapses. The trainer can use the same ploy in raising other issues, such as social embarrassment, that might accompany self-monitoring, for example, if others comment about the client's surreptitiously recording. The trainer and the client can discuss and role-play how the client might respond in such situations. Another major source of noncompliance with self-monitoring that can be anticipated is the client's mood, which could make the effort of recording seem like a real chore, a burden. Feelings of futility and hopelessness can interfere with self-monitoring. Using the imaginary client once again, the trainer can judiciously consider whether the client might have similar feelings, how these feelings might affect self-monitoring, and what can be done to handle such feelings.

The notion of *inoculation for failure* applies not only to self-monitoring exercises but also to all aspects of training (Marlatt & Gordon, 1984). In this way the trainer can help the client realize that even with the best of intentions unexpected lapses are likely. The trainer can help the client identify high-risk situations in which such faltering is possible and the variety of coping behaviors one can use in each situation. Such inoculation, or client preparation, nurtures the client's sense of control and minimizes "catastrophizing" thoughts and feelings when relapse occurs. The main principle behind such inoculation efforts is that adequate information about potential problems helps clients prepare alternative coping strategies rather than contributes to giving up. The client is encouraged to see such failures, and subsequently any backsliding, as signals to reexert control by reactivating the coping skills that were reviewed in training.

In summary, the request to the client to self-monitor is embedded in a clinical transaction of preparing the client for self-monitoring—giving the client the opportunity to suggest the procedure himself or herself, conducting a comprehension check, anticipating and subsuming possible reasons why he or she might not adhere, and actually practicing specific behaviors a client might employ in such situations. Throughout the discussion, the client is a collaborator sharing his or her feelings about the worth of the self-monitoring. As noted, the field of self-monitoring has focused too much on the mechanics of the self-assessment procedure, and it has failed to consider the larger clinical context in which it is embedded. As we shall see, these same concerns apply to each of the training techniques discussed in the next chapter.

Self-monitoring Exercises. If the trainer cannot have the client successfully engage in the self-monitoring exercise, then it is unlikely that the client will undertake more demanding exercises in subsequent phases of training. The following examples illustrate some of the ways clients have participated in generating self-monitoring procedures. For instance, one parent noted that she became particularly stressed with her children at dinner. Each simple no would seem to escalate into a heated confrontation.

> Don't talk with your mouth full. Use your napkin. No, don't throw peas at your brother. Don't say "yuck," you didn't even try it. Please use your fork when you eat your meat, not your spoon. Don't run away from the table before asking to be excused . . . and so on.

(Clearly such a litany of rules is enough to make parents want to eat alone!) The self-monitoring exercise asks her merely to keep track of when she said no to her children, imposing a variety of rules not only at dinner but throughout the course of a day. The goal was not to have her adopt a laissez faire attitude nor relinquish her socializing efforts, but to enlist her as a collaborator in identifying which are "necessary noes" and which are "unnecessary noes." In this way she could begin to collect data on the transactional nature of her stress. She was not merely the victim of her children's behavior, but also often affected by her own concerns and parenting style, which contributed to the escalation.

She even generated a fascinating little experiment that she conducted at a dinner party in order to better understand her particular needs for orderliness. She identified an attractive male guest and kept a mental checklist of the number of "etiquette rules" she felt he broke. Although she would not tolerate her son's breaking such rules, she would normally disregard such behaviors in adults. Could she not use similar techniques with her children to avoid or reduce stress? How did her own standards and critical stance affect the sense of stress she felt in child rearing? The self-monitoring exercise was a useful means for her to reassess the nature of her parenting stress. Moreover, the trainer explored with her other settings (e.g., on her job) in which she experienced similar feelings and thoughts. In this way, the client and the trainer began to explore whether specific current concerns played a role in contributing to her stress reactions. Such probes nurtured a self-inquiring attitude on the part of the client, so that her internal dialogue, which initially conveyed a sense of helplessness and hopelessness, thoughts of characterological self-blame, was changed to self-queries such as,

> What are the data? How are my reactions contributing to my stress? If I had these thoughts, what is the evidence for my conclusions? Or put more simply, how do I know he meant that by what he did? If I look at it this way, where will it lead me? Just how serious is. . . ? What exactly is the degree of harm to me if . . . ?

Such a self-inquiring attitude lays the groundwork for the client to reconceptualize the nature of her stress and her ability to cope. Another example of SIT trainers using self-monitoring in an innovative fashion is when they involve the client and his or her spouse in the exercise. In general, it is important to involve family members in the SIT program from the outset. A cooperative spouse can provide much-needed support and encouragement as well as information about the client's progress. The spouse can also act as a collaborator in collecting data about the nature of the client's stress reaction. For example, in the treatment of chronic pain patients, Turk et al. (1983) not only asked the patient to monitor his or her pain on a 6-point rating scale and in a pain diary but also asked the patient's spouse to keep track independently of the patient's pain.

Such spouse information often proves quite revealing when the patient and spouse are brought together to compare notes. The first thing that usually emerges is joint recognition that the patient's stress varies across situations and over time and that one's stress is not always at the highest level. The trainer can wonder aloud why it is that sometimes the stress is high and at other times it drops. What distinguishes these two situations? If one better understood such differences would that help to reduce the client's stress level? Might the client be able to work to increase the number and duration of such low-stress periods? What impact do one's reactions and the reactions of other family members have on the nature of the client's stress? A useful tool to help answer this last question is to ask the spouse to describe the feelings and thoughts that precede, accompany, and follow the client's stress experience. The trainer can then question whether the client was indeed aware of the spouse's reactions. How could he or she tell what the reactions were and what impact they had on the client's stress level? Was the spouse aware of this . . . and so forth? How would life be different for both the client and spouse if the client's stress reaction (anger outbursts, pain, depression, etc.) did not occur?

As the discussion evolves, the trainer is carefully assessing whether the spouse can be viewed as an important social support or whether particular hidden agendas on the part of the spouse can operate as a source for sabotaging the stress management efforts. It is not being suggested, however, that all clients who are candidates for SIT require marital counseling or that their stress reactions are being maintained by a spouse or other family members or peers. In some instances, however, it is important to enlist significant others to participate in the collaborative effort. Likely, such spouse involvement will be of more relevance in a clinical setting than in a work setting. But even in such work settings (e.g., those of a police officer or teachers) one cannot readily segmentalize various sources of stress.

Finally, one cautionary note needs to be raised about the way in which trainers describe the self-monitoring task to clients. Some trainers have spoken of the self-monitoring task as a "homework assignment." The term *homework* often has surplus meaning, bringing to mind teacher-student relationships, with the client seeing himself or herself in a subservient role rather than as a joint partner in a collaborative venture.

I remember a client I saw when I first began SIT training who was quite stressed and very depressed. I had carefully laid the groundwork for her to self-monitor the stressful situations in which she became depressed. Inadvertently, I characterized the effort as a homework assignment. When she returned the next week she had complied with the request, but what was most interesting was the manner in which she discussed her efforts. She kept asking if she got it right. Was that what I wanted? And so forth. It soon became apparent to me that calling it homework had triggered her sense of having to please the "teacher." I soon reflected on her style and not on the content of her self-monitoring. Her desire to please not only the therapist but also others became the focus of attention. The homework assignment permitted an examination of the client's current concerns and their impact on her stress reactions. Often the manner in which the client discusses the homework assignment, his or her resistance in complying, and the like can be more informative than the specific content of the self-monitoring exercise itself.

Behavioral Assessments

Another useful source of information to aid the reconceptualization process is behavioral assessments in real life, in the clinic, or in the laboratory. SIT trainers have conducted in vivo behavioral assessments with such populations as hospitalized patients about to undergo noxious medical examinations, athletes preparing for sports competition, police officers undergoing stressful role-playing situations, pain patients experiencing experimentally induced pain. Such enactive experiences have been successfully supplemented with ongoing cognitive assessments and videotaping, which can be subsequently replayed to clients so they can report (on a post hoc basis) the subjective experiences they had during the behavioral sample. Such (re)constructions help clients appreciate their own contributions to their stress reactions. Moreover, such behavioral assessments help in determining whether the client's inability to cope is a reflection of an inadequate repertoire (not capable of executing responses effectively) or of internally and/or externally mediated interferences.

In some instances, clients could be encouraged to undertake "personal experiments" whereby they can actively seek out or even generate data. For example, if stressed teachers feel there is "little or nothing" they can do on the job to reduce stress, a mini-experiment could be collaboratively agreed upon whereby the client might try to behave differently toward others, to see what happens. These preplanned experiments are often designed with a view to generating data that will disconfirm hypotheses held by the client. It is important to appreciate that each of the guidelines offered earlier about homework (i.e., preparing the client, providing a rationale, planning carefully, anticipating and subsuming failures) applies in the case of these mini-experiments. Often, it is necessary to encourage the client to run several trials of the mini-experiment, in order to ensure a fair test.

Psychological Testing

Finally, a number of standardized psychological tests, as well as those that can be tailored to the specific population, can be quite helpful in better understanding the nature of the client's stress. Obviously, the specific measures to be chosen vary with the demands of the specific population. For example, in cases of pain, anger control, depression, anxiety, patient-specific questionnaires, self-report scales, self-efficacy and expectation measures have been developed. Similarly, specific stress assessment measures have been developed for various occupational groups (teachers, police officers, military recruits) and target populations (parents of babies suffering from sudden infant death syndrome, cancer patients, unemployed individuals, and so forth). In general, efforts at assessing stress reactions have moved away from omnibus personality tests (e.g., projectives, self-report batteries) to very specific target assessments.

The point to be underscored is that psychological testing can be quite useful in SIT, especially those measures that provide information about the client's stress reactions such as amount and degree of intrusive ideation, ways of coping, and nature of social support. For each measure, the client is seen as a collaborator, reviewing the rationale, nature, and results of the testing with the trainer. In fact, the data from the various sources (interviewing, imagery reconstruction, self-monitoring, behavioral observations, cognitive assessment, mini-experiments, and psychological testing) are reviewed with the client in order to diagnose the nature of his or her stress and to discuss what needs to be done to change.

Moreover, there is a need to assess not only the individual but also, wherever appropriate and possible, the nature of the client's social environment. Moos (1974) has highlighted the value of assessing the client's social climate and occupational ambiance. If one object of SIT is to make clients better problem solvers, then such environmental assessments can help them in considering either individual and/or group direct-action coping responses to deal with the source of their stress.

THE RECONCEPTUALIZATION PROCESS

The first phase of SIT concludes with the trainer's offering a conceptual model or a reconceptualization of the client's stress. Clients enter training with some notions or implicit models concerning their stress. An important feature of SIT is to help them reconceptualize their stress in more benign terms that are amenable to change. In fact, inherent in all treatments is some explanation or conceptual model that therapists or trainers use. Therapists do *not* just "do things" to clients. They invariably offer some rationale for what they are doing and why. The reconceptualization process serves several crucial purposes:

1. Provides a means of integrating the various sources of information and a means of conveying the transactional nature of stress and coping (e.g., fostering an increased awareness of the role of appraisal processes);
2. Translates the client's symptoms (bodily complaints, thoughts, feelings, maladaptive behaviors) into specific difficulties that can be pinpointed as addressable problems rather than as overwhelming, hopeless, undifferentiated, and uncontrollable;
3. Recasts the client's stress into terms that are amenable to solutions, or that one can accept, or in which one can find meaning;
4. Proposes that the client's stress goes through various stages and is in part under his or her own control;
5. Prepares the client for interventions contained within the treatment regimen. As the client views (or reframes) his or her stress from a transactional perspective, it leads naturally to the client's suggesting specific forms of intervention;
6. Creates a positive expectancy that the treatments being offered are indeed appropriate for the client's problems.

As with the other features of SIT, the conceptual model is presented in a low-key style, using the client's own data as a means of reframing the nature of his or her stress reactions. Put another way, the trainer has paid his or her dues, listening attentively and probing methodically. It is now time for the trainer to use this information the way a lawyer prepares a brief, in order to help the client reconceptualize stress and his or her ability to cope. Throughout the presentation, the trainer should check out each point with the client. In short, the conceptual model is not offered as a hard sell which could contribute to client resistance and psychological reactance. Rather, the client is once again viewed as a collaborator providing his or her own suggestions about how things go together.

The conceptual phase is thus designed to facilitate a translation process. Many stressed clients enter training with a confused understanding of their problems, feeling victimized by circumstances, feelings, and thoughts over which they feel they can exert little or no control. They often fail to appreciate how their own reactions, the way they appraise events, and their own ability to cope, can inadvertently potentiate and exacerbate their stress. As they collect and review data from a variety of sources, they have an opportunity to reconstrue their stress. They begin to recognize how their own reactions cocreate difficulties and how a transactional model of stress and coping applies in their case. If their own reactions can contribute to the stress they experience, then perhaps there is indeed something they can do to control and change their stress. Thus, throughout both the assessment and the treatment stages of the intervention, stress is reconceptualized as being amenable to change.

The specific conceptual model presented depends of course on the presenting problem and the specific population. For example, SIT trainers have used Schachter's (1966) cognitive physiological model of emotion with anxious clients, Lang's (1968) tripartite model of fear with rape victims, Melzack and Wall's (1965) gate control theory of pain with pain patients, and Lazarus's (1981) transactional model of stress with Type A businessmen. What is critical about each model is not its scientific validity per se, but its credibility and plausibility to clients and its heuristic value in suggesting specific avenues of intervention.[3] Such models help clients develop a more differentiated view of their stress reactions. Instead of their stress (pain, anger, depression, boredom, anxiety) appearing to be an all-or-none process, the model conveys to clients that their stress varies across situations and over time and that it is made of different components that go through various phases.[4] For example, the trainer might state:

> As I listen to you describe your stress experience, it seems to me that there are a number of different things going on. Correct me if I am wrong or if I am missing something, but it seems that the stress you are experiencing is made of several components and that your reactions involve a series of phases or stages. These include preparing for the stressor, confronting and trying to handle stressful events, coping with feelings of being overwhelmed, and reflecting about your coping efforts.

At this point, the trainer conveys a conceptual model of stress, using the client's own descriptions, as gleaned from interviews, diaries, and other sources, to illustrate and document each of the proposed com-

[3]Often such models are reassuring to clients. For example, the pain patient who is suspicious of a psychological interpretation of his or her problem might feel reassured by the gate control model, which integrates both physical and psychological variables. Similarly, the tripartite model of fear facilitates the reattribution process of rape victims, because it emphasizes the conditioning of "automatic" learned reactions that can be "reconditioned" and unlearned. These models emphasize ongoing transactional processes rather than characterological traits that imply basic personal inadequacies. Stress is a process, and such processes can be changed.

[4]Space does not permit a detailed account of the various conceptual models that have been offered in SIT. The interested reader should see Meichenbaum (1977), Novaco (1977a), and Turk et al. (1983) for further descriptions of the reconceptualization process.

ponents and phases. Throughout, the client acts as a collaborator in a participatory relationship with the trainer in conducting the reconceptualization process. The client (and sometimes a significant other) is encouraged to offer examples and provide feedback. The goal of the reconceptualization process is to recast the client's stress experience in terms that imply hope and resourcefulness. Instead of the client's viewing his or her stress in global terms, the trainer works with the client to develop a more differentiated view—one that "chunks" stress into manageable units the client can influence. Once again, it is worth reiterating that the reconceptualization process is not a didactic presentation or a lecture. Rather, it is a Socratic-type dialogue always using the client's own feelings, thoughts, and behavior and others' reactions, which provide consensual validation for the model being presented. For example, the trainer can state:

> As I listen to you describe your stress, it seems as if it goes through, what shall we call it, different phases, stages. I have the sense, and correct me if I am wrong, that there are times when you can almost *prepare* yourself for the stress. For example, Don, when you were coming home, you indicated that you wondered if your wife was going to go out and what the evening would bring. Or the time when the departmental meeting resulted in your becoming so stressed. Clearly, not all stressful events have a preparatory phase, but it does seem that you do have some sense of what are the high-risk situations, when your "fuse is short," when you are prone to becoming stressed.

At this point, the trainer and the client consider examples of such high-risk situations, their similarities and differences, and the prodromal cues that the client can use to know when he or she is becoming stressed. One goal of the reconceptualization process is to help clients become aware of low-intensity cues. It is easier to interrupt or short-circuit the stress cycle in its earlier stages than when the client is in the "heat of the battle." If the client has a plan and well-rehearsed coping techniques, then he or she can use them at the various stages of the stress reaction. In this spirit, the trainer continues,

> A second phase of your stress is when you are already *confronting* the stressful event. Things are building up, you are feeling taxed. You have so many things to do—grade the exams, the grant proposal is due, put the kids to bed. Only if you can relax for an hour, perhaps watch a television program. What was that? "Oh no, I don't believe it, Dave's running in the tub again." You feel the stress building in the muscles in the arms, the heavy breathing. You have to confront and try to handle the stressful event.

Once again, the trainer uses the client's behavior to illustrate a specific phase of the stress reaction, eliciting other examples where the client's appraisal processes play a critical role in influencing the nature of stress. The trainer continues,

> A third phase of stress, and one that you sometimes experience, is what I shall call *critical moments* when you are feeling overwhelmed, very stressed. All hell has broken out—"Oh no, the door knob hit her eye, he fell in the tub, the baby's crying, where's the ruler!" On a 10-point scale of stress, you're 12, if not higher. We have all had such reactions. We have all encountered such critical moments in our lives.

> Moreover, such critical moments often don't end there. We often reflect afterward on such stressful incidents, as we continue to dwell upon such incidents, perpetuating them further as we talk to ourselves and to others. This is the phase when you *reflect* about how you coped or failed to cope with your stress. At these points you consider how things went, and how you handled your stress.

The trainer at this point can pause for mutual examination of the ways in which the client's thinking style (e.g., penchant to catastrophize or to be perfectionistic) influences her or his feelings and behavior. The trainer can also raise a question about the impact of such reactions on the client's handling of future stressful events. The trainer's Columbo routine can help the client recognize the interdependence of stressful events, how specific current concerns cut across stressful events. The Socratic-type probes can help the client appreciate how the building of tension and the anticipation of events as personal threats rather than challenges contribute to the increase of stress.

If SIT is run on a group basis, the trainer can refer to examples offered by several of the participants. The trainer should ensure that the model is presented in lay terms at a level appropriate to the clients' understanding. The art of training is the ability to individually tailor the language, examples, and metaphors to the clients' backgrounds. The types of examples used with a rural farmer are probably quite different from those used with an urban business person; those with a macho male athlete, from those with a petite, withdrawn female. The style of offering the model is continuously interactive, with the trainer repeatedly checking each component with the client. Such phrases as the following foster such a collaborative effect:

Correct me if I am wrong.

Have I missed something?

Is this the way you see it?

Let me see if this fits with your view.

The aim is not to convert the client to a "true" conception of his or her problem, but to encourage the client to adapt a way of looking at stress that nurtures change. Throughout, the trainer solicits the client's feedback, permits interruptions, and reads the client's reactions to the conceptualization effort, in order to ensure a fit between the client's conceptualization of his or her problem and the rationale of the training being offered. This is nicely illustrated in the work with pain patients. Many pain patients have a conception of illness that is based on an acute disease model (Leventhal, Meyer, & Nerenz, 1980). Pain is viewed as a primary symptom being caused by something discrete and out of the patient's direct control (e.g., a pathogen, an injury). Pain is expected to be susceptible to specific medical treatments that will exert their beneficial effects in a relatively brief period of time (viz., "there is a pill for every ill"). According to this model, things are done to the patient, and the patient has little or no role in potentiating or eliminating the pain. As Turk, Holzman, and Kerns (1985) note, the acute disease model places minimal responsibility on the patient and encourages and rewards passivity. The acute disease model conveys the message that the client's pain is largely beyond his or her ability to change and out of his or her control. The reconceptualization process is designed to help clients develop a self-management perspective by helping them collect and then evaluate data that implicate the role of psychological factors in the experiences of pain. The central message throughout the treatment, from the initial contact, is that patients are not helpless in dealing with their pain. The reconceptualization process encourages patients to adopt a problem-solving set and to develop a sense of resourcefulness instead of feelings of helplessness. In short, there is a need to establish a therapeutic alliance. The reconceptualization process plays a critical role in this effort.

The reconceptualization process evolves gradually, serving as a framework that is refined continuously over the course of training. In some instances, SIT trainers have attempted to consolidate the reconceptualization process by giving the client reading material that illustrates other examples of the conceptual model. For example, patient materials have been developed for such problems as anger control, depression, stress, pain, and unassertiveness (Linehan & Egan, 1983; Meichenbaum, 1983; Novaco, 1975; Rodin, 1983; Rush, 1983; Turk et al., 1983), as well as for specific stressed populations (see Meichenbaum & Jaremko, 1983).

Even a seemingly innocuous feature such as giving clients something to read should be treated with care by SIT trainers. Once again, the trainer anticipates and subsumes potential client resistance in the presentation.

Because we discussed the various features of your stress, I thought it might be both interesting and helpful for you to read some material about your stress between now and next time. I have a brief pamphlet (book) that describes other clients who have also had similar stressful reactions and some of the things they did to handle them. Now, before you read this material, I want to remind you that every client is unique and each person's problems differ. Thus, in some instances you will read something that fits well with your own experience, but, in other instances, you may disagree with what you read. That is fine. In fact, we can spend some time next week examining what does and what does not work in your situation.

The trainer tries to anticipate the fact that the client might disagree and dismiss certain features of the biblio-material, but, by giving the client license, indeed encouraging such critical appraisal, the trainer tries to ensure that the rejection of one aspect of the material does not lead to total rejection of the treatment program. The central premise is to subsume into the conceptual model each of the possible reasons why clients will not adhere to the treatment.

SUMMARY

The major objective of the first phase is to set the stage for subsequent interventions, by establishing a collaborative working relationship between client(s) and trainer. The trainer uses a variety of means including interview, imagery recall, self-monitoring, behavioral assessments, and psychological testing to collect information about the nature of the client's stress. This information provides the client with a reconceptualization of his or her stress reactions. The reconceptualization process is sometimes supplemented with biblio-material. This chapter highlighted the clinical guidelines and trainer style needed to enlist collaboration and avoid client resistance and treatment nonadherence.

Chapter 5
Skills Acquisition and Rehearsal Phase

The description of the initial conceptualization phase in chapter 4 reveals that a great deal transpires before any specific coping skills are explicitly taught and rehearsed. The initial phase serves several important goals including the analysis of presenting problems (nature of clients' stress and coping); the enlisting of clients as collaborators, whereby they can analyze their stress autonomously; and the laying of a groundwork for subsequent training.

The objective of the second phase of SIT is to ensure that the client develops the capacity to effectively execute coping responses.[1] As in the previous phase, the client is viewed as a collaborator in this effort. What suggestions does the client have about ways to reduce and avoid stress? What has the client tried in the past that has worked or failed? Such probes are designed to tap the client's attitudes and expectations about specific stress management procedures. For example, clients may indicate that they have tried relaxation, assertiveness, not thinking about a stressful event, or keeping busy. However, none of these work. As the client describes such efforts at coping, the trainer is listening and probing about such variables as the specific type of coping, the criteria used for success, the duration and timing of the efforts, reactions to failure, and so forth. In short, a central guideline in this second phase of training is that the trainer repeatedly assesses the client's internal dialogue about each training procedure. It is important for the trainer to have information about the client's attitudes and expectations for each particular training technique that is introduced. If clients hold a negative set or a dubious attitude about one element of the training regimen, the credibility of the entire pro-

---

[1]Component analysis studies of SIT by Horan, Hackett, Buchanan, Stone, and Demchik-Stone (1977) and Vallis (1984) indicated that the skills acquisition phase plays a critical role. When this phase is dropped, the efficacy of SIT is significantly lowered. There is also some suggestion that the skills acquisition phase is mediated by increased use of relaxation and/or by a decrease in catastrophizing.

gram can be lessened, and resistance and nonadherence could increase. Once the trainer appreciates the client's concerns, then he or she can anticipate and subsume them into the training rationale for each coping procedure. The trainer can also highlight any distinctions between what the client has tried in the past and what is being suggested currently.

The coping skills that are taught vary with the specific population and with the goals of training. The coping repertoire is tailored to the needs of the specific population. For example, SIT training for pain patients might include attentional control training; whereas, for anger-control patients, communication skills might be most appropriate. For victim populations, denial processes might be useful early in training, to be supplemented with problem solving and cognitive restructuring later on in training. Unfortunately, at this stage in the development of SIT, the literature does not suggest what specific coping techniques are best suited for each population, nor the order in which they should be taught. This is partly due to the fact that our research efforts have focused on individuals who do not cope with stress effectively. We have little information about how people adaptively cope with stress. Given this limited empirical base, one must be cautious about so-called "formulas" for coping. The training approach adopted by SIT is to offer the variety of coping techniques in a cafeteria style, whereby clients can experiment in determining what works best for them. The goal is to nurture a flexible coping repertoire and to work with clients in a collaborative fashion, in order to select, test, and assess the merits of various coping procedures.

The coping techniques to be taught include what Lazarus and Launier (1978) called *instrumental* (problem-focused) and *palliative* (emotion-regulation) coping techniques. Included under instrumental coping are such techniques as information gathering, problem solving, communication and social skills training, time management, life-style changes such as reassessing priorities, mobilizing supports, and direct action efforts designed to change the environmental demands or alter stressful situations and transactions.

The instrumental coping skills are tailored to the needs and environmental demands of a specific population. For example, stressed parents might receive specific training in parenting skills. In such cases, enactive training of relevant coping techniques by means of modeling, practice, and feedback, initially in the clinic or lab and then gradually in vivo, can be of value.

Under palliative coping are included a number of techniques designed to relieve distress and foster emotion-regulation. The palliative techniques include taking perspective such as engaging in social comparisons and searching for meaning, diverting attention, denial, expressing affect, and training in relaxation. These coping techniques are most relevant when a stressful or aversive situation can be neither altered nor avoided (e.g., life-threatening illness, having been victimized).

We will consider these problem-focused and emotion-regulation coping techniques shortly. At this time it is important to appreciate that the goal of training is to nurture a flexible, integrated coping repertoire that is situationally sensitive to the full range of stressful transactions. In some instances clients already have such coping skills in their repertoires, and such skills should be consolidated; whereas, in other instances, explicit training might be required. In either case, the specific techniques should emerge from the (re)conceptualization process.

The one caution is that the trainer should not overwhelm clients with the plethora of coping options. Such a high-powered presentation could prove stress engendering. Clinical skill is needed to nurture clients' sense of self-management and belief in their ability to exercise control. Clients are told that the object of training is not to totally remove stress but to use their stress constructively—to view it as a challenge, an opportunity, a problem to be solved.

RELAXATION TRAINING

Although the order in which coping techniques are considered in SIT has varied, most trainers begin with relaxation training, because it is readily learned by almost all clients and has a good deal of face validity. A number of diverse procedures have been used to teach relaxation. However, no one approach appears to be more beneficial than any other. Moreover, specific treatment manuals and client-assisted relaxation audiotapes are available and will not be reproduced in this text. A specific relaxation protocol can be found in Turk et al. (1983). The 1984 book by Woolfolk and Lehrer described the various relaxation procedures. The discussion here focuses on clinical guidelines for conducting relaxation training.

Clinical Guidelines

First, the introduction of relaxation should grow out of the conceptualization process. The trainer can refer to the client's bodily signs of physical tenseness. If in fact such tenseness exacerbates stress, then it is not a big step for the client to suggest that relaxation can help her or him reduce stress. The trainer then provides a rationale for the specific relaxation procedure to be used. Reference is made to a stress-tension cycle—how occupying one's attention can short-circuit stress, how relaxation can reduce anxiety because it represents something clients can do to exert control, how relaxation and tension are incompatible states, and, finally, how unwinding after a stressful experience can be therapeutic. (See Frankenhaeuser, 1981, for a discussion of the physiological mechanisms underlying the ability to unwind or to return to physiological baseline following a stressful event. Turk et al., 1983, provided a detailed presentation of the relaxation rationale.)

Also highlighted is the fact that one can relax not only by tensing and releasing muscle groups or by means of some passive activity such as meditation, but also by means of absorbing activities such as walking, swimming, knitting, gardening, ventilating to others, and so forth. All too often trainers fail to underline the fact that relaxation is as much a state of mind as it is a physical state. One teacher noted that the way she copes with stress is "to kiss the bricks good-bye" once she leaves school.

Second, as noted previously, there is a need to tap the client's previous experience with and expectations concerning relaxation. In some instances, clients have viewed relaxation as a mere "mind game," or they have had concerns about using relaxation because they felt that mental alertness was required on their jobs. Such concerns can be dealt with accordingly. In the first instance, cue-controlled biofeedback[2] can be used to assist relaxation training. The SIT trainer can capitalize on the placebo value of biofeedback, as the stressed client now feels that the trainer has employed a treatment procedure (biofeedback) that is commensurate with the seriousness of the client's problems. The trainer must be sensitive to not only the specifics of the training procedure but also the client's internal dialogue about its use. In the instance where a client has a concern about the supposed incompatibility of alertness and relaxation, the trainer can indicate that relaxation training is designed to help the client selectively focus attention while remaining both relaxed and vigilant. Thus, it is important for the trainer not only to focus on the specifics of the relaxation training, but also to discuss with a client what it means to be relaxed and how the client has to give himself or herself permission to relax. The client has to learn that it is not a waste of time to learn to relax.

The trainer should help the client self-disclose his or her concerns about each training procedure. In this way the trainer can individually tailor the discussion to the client's specific concerns.

Third, when relaxation is introduced, it is offered as an active coping

---

[2]Space does not permit a consideration of biofeedback training. It is worth noting, however, that recent studies by Holroyd and his colleagues indicate that cognitive changes induced by performance feedback (viz., reduction in negative ideation, changes in self-efficacy expectancies and coping responses to stress) contribute to the effectiveness of biofeedback (Holroyd et al., in press). It is not primarily reductions in bodily activities that mediate the efficacy of biofeedback, but the changes in how individuals appraise and cope with stressful events. These findings have important implications as to how biofeedback should be used in stress management programs (see Lazarus, 1975; Meichenbaum, 1976; Turk et al., 1983).

skill—one which requires practice (Goldfried, 1977). As Woolfolk and Lehrer (1984) noted, there is a need to convey to a client that the amount of gain is tied to how much one practices. The trainer should convey: ''It won't work if you don't do it.'' The trainer can also draw an analogy with the role practice plays in athletics or in artistic endeavors. Moreover, the trainer can include within the training any potential problems a client might have. For example, if the trainer senses that the client is concerned about his or her mind wandering during the relaxation exercise, the trainer can suggest that the ability to let one's mind wander is a sign that the individual is in fact becoming more and more relaxed. Because relaxation is a skill that requires practice, the trainer discusses with the client why, when, and how such practice will be conducted. In addition, there is a need to anticipate and subsume any problems a client might have in carrying out the homework assignment. The trainer should underscore the fact that, because relaxation is a skill, the client should *not* expect to see sudden large changes but a gradual improvement in coping ability. The trainer should ensure that the client does not have unrealistically high expectations about the training, as if one technique such as relaxation would, in a brief period of time, rid him or her of the debilitating effects of stress. The object is to manage, not eradicate, stress. The acquisition of such coping skills is never a steady and smooth process.

Fourth, a number of different relaxation procedures, such as pleasant personal relaxation images, breathing exercises, and cognitive cue-controlling procedures, have been used as supplements to Jacobsonian-type muscular relaxation exercises (see Turk et al., 1983, for a description of these various techniques). In fact, it is important to appreciate that clients can be muscularly relaxed yet automatically aroused, which suggests the need to supplement the muscular relaxation procedure.

Fifth, there is a need to discuss specific ways in which the client will use the relaxation coping skill in anticipation of stressful situations, especially when low-intensity cues are evident. The trainer must not assume that the client will readily apply (or generalize) the procedures across situations. Such generalization needs to be built into the training regimen. For example, in an institutional setting, not just the client has been trained in relaxation training, so has the client's counselor. Both client and counselor received joint relaxation training, so that the counselor could subsequently model and cue the client on the ward on when and how to use relaxation as a coping device and could model the use of relaxation to control his or her own reactions. Throughout, the counselor acted as a coping model. In this way, relaxation training was not merely a technique taught to the client in weekly sessions. It was also an active coping response that the client encountered daily.

Finally, there is a need to ensure that the client reviews the consequences of his or her coping efforts and makes self-attributions for improvement. The trainer can once again adopt a Columbo routine, asking the client to explain how he or she was able to manage stress by means of the relaxation response. SIT trainers can even ask clients to imagine themselves in various stress and conflict situations and describe how they would use the relaxation procedures to control their reactions. (We will consider the imagery procedure in more detail in the next chapter.)

The discussion of these clinical guidelines indicates that any specific coping procedure such as relaxation training is couched within an ongoing client-trainer relationship. There is a need to provide a rationale, to discuss issues of practice, generalization, and self-attribution over and above the specific training procedure.

COGNITIVE STRATEGIES

As noted in the reconceptualization process, one aspect of the client's stress is reflected in the physical tenseness and bodily arousal the client experienced. Physical and mental relaxation were designed to help clients control such distress. Another feature of the client's stress was the nature of his or her accompanying thoughts and feelings. To control the impact of such cognitive and affective processes, SIT employs a number of cognitive procedures including cognitive restructuring, problem solving, and guided self-dialogue. In considering each of these cognitive interventions, it is important to underscore the fact that cognitions should not be viewed as entities antecedent to other psychological or physiological processes. Instead, cognition should be viewed as a set of relationships that are interdependent on other processes. Cognitive interventions should be viewed as only one of several possible points of entry into what are essentially interrelated processes (emotions, physiological reactions, behavior, social consequences).

The first of the cognitive interventions we will consider is cognitive restructuring, which is designed to make clients aware of the role cognitions and emotions play in potentiating and maintaining stress. Consistent with the objective of establishing a collaborative approach whereby clients can reframe the nature of their stress, the cognitive restructuring approach used in SIT is based on Aaron Beck's work on cognitive therapy.

Even though the specific components of cognitive therapy have been described elsewhere (Beck et al., 1979), the major features will be briefly reviewed here, especially in regard to treating stress-related problems. The core techniques of cognitive therapy include:

1. Eliciting the client's thoughts, feelings, and interpretation of events;
2. Gathering evidence with the client for or against such interpretations;

3. Setting up personal experiments (homework) to test the validity of the interpretations and to gather more data for discussion.

To accomplish these objectives, the trainer is quite active, focusing on the here and now. The trainer does not regard himself or herself as knowing the answers (as the expert). Instead, the trainer acts as a collaborator with the client in finding out answers. This joint inquiry by trainer and client has been called *collaborative empiricism* by Hollon and Beck (1979). The procedure consists of framing the client's conclusion as a hypothesis, which is then jointly investigated.

The first task in cognitive therapy has been called *thought catching*, and it is designed to help stressed clients become aware of the automatic thoughts, images, and accompanying feelings they have when they are stressed. Beck (1963) used the term *automatic thoughts* to describe discrete specific thoughts clients have that occur very rapidly, seemingly unprompted by events (out of the blue), and are not the result of "directed" thinking. They are specific in content, provide interpretation of events, and often include predictions about situations. They can occur outside a person's awareness. When individuals do notice them, they are usually viewed as indisputable and incontrovertible facts or truths. The object of this exercise in increased self-awareness is to help clients recognize that their thoughts and conclusions are often inferences, not facts, and that the way they process information is fallible and subject to cognitive distortion. Table 5.1 lists some of the automatic thoughts that stressed clients have offered.

In reading over this list of automatic thoughts, it is important to ap-

Table 5.1. Examples of Negative,
Stress-engendering, Automatic Thoughts

It is such an effort to do anything.
I'm not as good as others.
Everything is futile.
The future is just one string of problems.
I have only made mistakes in the past.
Everything I do turns out badly.
There is no one I can turn to.
Life has no meaning.
The future is hopeless.
These thoughts (or feelings) just overwhelm me.
There is nothing I can do to control them.
I let them down. It's all my fault.

---

preciate that it is not the presence of such thoughts per se that represents the problem, but rather that such negative (often absolutistic) ideation triggers further negative dysfunctional feelings and stress-engendering behavior, with their accompanying consequences. This pattern leads subsequently to further negative ideation. A vicious cycle develops, because stressed individuals are less likely to spontaneously interrupt or permit others to interrupt their stress-engendering pattern. Parenthetically, it should be noted that individuals who "cope well"[3] with stress can also have negative stress-engendering thoughts; but in their case such ideation is open to interruption and they spontaneously employ coping responses such as social comparison, denial, and problem solving (Meichenbaum, Henshaw, & Himel, 1982).

The SIT trainer helps clients recognize the occurrence and impact of their automatic thoughts and feelings. As the trainer probes for the meanings of such thoughts, the client begins to question the validity of his or her conclusions. Automatic thoughts become hypotheses worthy of testing, rather than God-given assertions or truths. To accomplish these tasks, a number of clinical techniques are used.

First, the trainer might use the clinical interview as a means of having clients attend to such automatic thoughts. Such probes as the following might be helpful:

> What thoughts were running through your head just before you came in to see me? Do you have similar thoughts and feelings in stressful situations at home?
>
> What do you think will happen in such situations?
>
> What do you picture happening?
>
> What are you saying to yourself in that situation?
>
> Then what?
>
> How do you know that that will indeed happen?
>
> What is the evidence of a threat?
>
> How serious is it?
>
> What coping resources are available?

Such questions are designed to pull forth the client's automatic thoughts (expectations, attributions, self-statements), which can then be examined under the scrutiny of Columbo-like probes.

---

[3]The notion of a "good" versus a "poor" coper can be misleading. As Silver and Wortman (1980) observed, various indexes of coping (self-report, behavioral indices, physiological reactions) often do not correlate highly, suggesting that coping is a multidimensional concept. Thus, the search for correlates of good coping can be complicated by the index of coping that one uses.

In addition, the trainer develops an "attuned ear" for the client's use of the words *must, should, always, never*.[4] After the client has been able to tell his or her "tale of woe" or describe his or her stress, the trainer helps the client reframe the stress reactions. When the client makes such statements as "What's the use? I'll never be able to find meaning in life! My whole life is affected," the trainer can do one of four things.

First, decide not to respond, not interrupting the client.

Second, respond to the feeling reflected by such a statement as "At times I feel it's hopeless, that there is no use going on, given what has happened to me."

Third, focus on the content of what is being said. The trainer can be a "plucker," pulling a few words out of the client's statements and reflecting these back to the client so that he or she can reconsider them. For example, the trainer could ask, "Never, *never* find meaning?" or "Your *whole* life is affected?" In this way, the trainer attempts to make the client aware of the absolutistic nature of his or her thinking. At times it is sufficient to merely highlight the client's cognitive style without pursuing it further until the client offers several examples of such thinking processes. At this point, the trainer can juxtapose such data as follows:

Never, never find meaning.

You're a *complete* failure because you didn't do more.

You *can't do anything* to control how you feel.

There is no hope.

Fourth, explore with the client the impact of such thoughts on how the client feels and behaves. The trainer could ask the client, "How do you feel when you say, 'What's the use? I'll never be able to find meaning in life?'" It is important when doing this that the trainer not belittle the client's problem but rather rephrase it. For example, consider the following trainer-client example:

Trainer: When you say to yourself, "What's the use? You'll never be able to find meaning. Your whole life is affected," how does it leave you feeling?

Client: Hopeless . . . helpless . . . sad.

Trainer: How true do you think it really is that your stress affects everything in your life?

Client: It seems to affect everything. I'll never get over it.

Trainer: I would like to ask you to do something a bit unusual such as indicate how much you believe your statement, "It always affects everything.

[4]Karen Horney (1950) has described the "tyranny of shoulds" that can exacerbate stress, and Albert Ellis (1962) has described the "musturbation" process ("I *must* do this") that stress clients engage in.

I'll never be able to find meaning." What would your rating be, let's
say, on a 0% to 100% scale, where 100% is absolute belief?

Client: You mean you want me to tell you how much I actually believe what
I say to myself.

Trainer: How much do you believe that "stress affects everything"?

Client: Right now, I would say 100%.

Trainer: Can you tell me about a time when your stress affected your whole
life?

Client: (Client relates example.)

Trainer: Are there any times when you felt stressed, but it seemed that your
whole life didn't fall apart?

Client: Well, I guess there have been times when I have pulled myself together.

Trainer: Really. Can you offer an example of such an instance where you felt
stressed but were able to pull yourself together.

Client: (Client is encouraged to report specific examples.)

Trainer: So it seems that at some times you do in fact manage to cope pretty
well . . . At the start of this discussion you said there was no meaning,
your whole life was affected, you could't cope with anything. I am wondering how much you believe this statement now.

Client: I don't know. It's still pretty bad, maybe 50%.

As Beck et al. (1979) noted, clients rarely reality test in this fashion as
they selectively attend to negative stress-engendering thoughts. The trainer has to repeat this same process again and again throughout training
before the client spontaneously begins to engage in such self-inquiry.

In this way, the trainer attempts to help clients gain distance from and
look at their thoughts more objectively, thus appreciating the effect automatic thoughts have on feelings and behaviors. For example, the trainer
might state:

> In this session we talked about several recent incidents in which you felt
> stressed and upset. We also observed the kinds of things that ran through
> your mind and the impact they had on your feelings and behavior. (Trainer
> gives examples.) In fact, it is rare that people feel stress without there being
> a thought behind it. In the coming week I would like you to test out whether
> this in fact occurs for you by asking you to keep track of the automatic
> thoughts you have when you become stressed.

As noted in our earlier discussion on self-monitoring, there is a need
for the trainer to explain the nature of the recording process, to perform
a comprehension check, to discuss possible obstacles, and to give the client
an opportunity to voice concerns and doubts about the procedure.

After the noting and recording of particular cognitions, the next step
is to evaluate them logically. For example, the trainer can ask clients for
evidence that their automatic thoughts are indeed valid. The trainer can
encourage clients to perform personal experiments (homework assignments) to test specific hypotheses. Clients are encouraged to test out their

expectations of how others will react. Often, stressed individuals become egocentric, and cognitive therapy is designed to help them decenter their perceptions, taking the perspective of others into account.

Cognitive therapists such as Beck (1984) have also asked clients to introduce a 0 to 100 scale into their appraisals of situations. In order to convey to clients that their appraisal of stressful events is relative, not absolute, the trainer asks clients, "What was the worst experience you ever had?" If the client rates that incident 100, then how does the client view the present stressful situation? Such techniques help clients maintain a sense of proportion. Moreover, clients are encouraged to postpone acting on their automatic thoughts until they have had a chance to review the bases for their conclusions. They are encouraged to rate the probabilities of the possible consequences. Such judgments can help undercut the perceived seriousness of possible outcomes.

In summary, we see that much clinical skill is needed in determining which of the four options to employ. Should the trainer merely listen attentively, empathically reflect feelings, highlight cognitive style, or consider the impact of automatic thoughts on the client's feelings and behavior? Each of these options is called for at some point in training. Obviously, the length and goals of training and the nature of the client population play an important role in answering this question.

In general, my own technique is to follow the four steps in the order presented, so that examination of the impact of thoughts on feelings does not occur until a safe, trusting relationship has been established through listening attentively and reflecting empathically. Also, before examination of the question of the impact of the client's thoughts, several examples of the client's automatic thoughts should have been offered both within the training session and descriptions of automatic thoughts experienced in vivo. The sequence and timing of such clinical efforts are important. The trainer's being too forceful, too didactic, too intrusive, can contribute to client resistance and cause the client to back off. In short, the groundwork must be laid if the client and trainer are to meet the client's automatic thoughts head on, thus challenging their validity. The trainer emphasizes a data-gathering approach throughout rather than a success/failure outlook. Instead of challenging the client's conclusions, the trainer encourages the client to "try it out and see how far you get." The trainer could note that he or she is not sure if what the client proposes is more or less difficult than the client imagines. The trainer conveys ignorance of exactly what the outcome will be. "Is it as bad as it seems? Is there anything to be done?" asks the trainer in a manner that would make Columbo proud.

The next step in the cognitive restructuring process is for clients to begin to notice the way they tend to think about situations (what Beck has described as *cognitive errors*). These errors include the tendency to overgeneralize, to see things in black-and-white terms, to catastrophize, to selectively focus on one aspect of an event and attribute undue significance to it, and to jump to conclusions. The goal is to help clients know when they are becoming stressed (preferably picking up low-intensity cues) and learn to ask themselves questions when they notice their stress. For example, the trainer can ask clients to examine the content of their self-statements, as in the case of decatastrophizing predictions and attributing responsibility.

> Well, let's suppose for the moment that the following did indeed occur (trainer offers example of client's worst fear). What would happen then?
>
> Just how much responsibility do you really have for this occurring?
>
> Could there be other reasons for X?
>
> How would you know that was the way he viewed it?
>
> Is it possible that there are other reasons for what happened?
>
> Is it as bad as it seems?
>
> How does that happening in fact cause you to be stressed?
>
> What would be the worst possible thing that could occur to you? Let's assume for the moment that the worst possible thing actually happened. What would happen then? Could you make some predictions? What thoughts and feelings would you have?

At this point the trainer could introduce the clinical technique offered by Ellis (1962):

> Let's say for the moment that what happened, that situation, is called A. And let's say that you became distressed, upset (trainer describes client's likely feelings and behavior). Let's call such reactions C. What I am trying to understand is How does situation A cause consequence C? What happened to B? What is the B—the thoughts, feelings, appraisal, meaning you had in that situation?

At this point the trainer can use his or her Columbo routine exploring with clients the various cognitive and emotional factors that mediate the stressful reaction. Moreover, clients and trainers can mutually explore other stressful situations, in order to determine if specific commonalities, themes, or schemata emerge.

With this as background, clients can be encouraged to challenge, reality test, look for evidence that supports or refutes predictions, and arrange for personal experiments to test the validity of their expectations. The types of questions the trainer asks provide a model for the clients, so they can begin to ask themselves:

> What exactly is at stake?
>
> Does this situation reflect a threat signaling potential harm, or a challenge, signaling an opportunity?

Do I have the resources to handle this situation?

How do I know that this will indeed happen?

What evidence do I have that this will happen?

Are there other ways of looking at the situation?

There are times when I don't do as well as I would like, but other times I do, so what are the differences?

Have I only had failures in situations in the past, or were there times I did okay?

What am I saying to myself right now?

What is the evidence for this conclusion?

Is there evidence that contradicts this conclusion?

Are there alternative explanations for how I am feeling?

The SIT trainer models the use of such self-inquiry throughout. For example, when a trainer reviews a client's weekly progress, the client invariably says, at some point, "It didn't work," referring to some homework assignment, personal experiment, or coping technique. Whenever I hear a client say, "It didn't work," the first thing I do is take a slow, deep breath and exhale slowly. Secondly, I say to myself, "Okay Don, earn your money." At which point, I call upon all the clinical acumen and experience I can muster, and I lean over to the client and I say, "It didn't work?" Note how much clinical savvy is required in this reflection, as one can emphasize the "*It*" or highlight "didn't work?" I am not being facetious, because much of the cognitive restructuring is indeed of this very nature. It is the task of both client and trainer to determine what the "it" entailed. What exactly did the client do in what situation, when, and so forth? Moreover, "didn't work" in what way? How would the client know if the coping effort did work? Is the client saying, "It will never work, what's the use, it's hopeless"? Such probes are designed to nurture a sense of self-analysis and problem solving.

The trainer is trying to nurture a cognitive style whereby the client turns certainties into possibilities. "What are the odds on this happening?" is a question that the trainer asks of the client and, in time, the client can ask of himself or herself. The trainer tries to make the client aware of absolutistic thinking, such as equating one mistake with total failure or employing overgeneralized labels, and learn to replace them with more relative terms. Such terms as *always* are more often appropriately phrased as *often; never* as *rarely; I must* as *I want; I need* as *I prefer; I can't* as *I would find it difficult*; and *I can never* as *In the past, I have been unable to*. This shift is not a simple matter of semantics or a lesson in logic, but a collaborative effort to help clients appreciate how their thinking style can exacerbate stress.

Even when the client states, "It doesn't work," the trainer can anticipate and subsume such reactions into the training by including an inoculation to failure and relapse. The trainer can say:

> With regard to the stress you are experiencing, there are a number of different things we can try and that you might find helpful. Some might prove useful, whereas others might not. Because every client is different and everybody's problems are unique, we will have to work together to determine what is best for you. As we do so, we might encounter failures, but such setbacks can prove both informative and helpful.
>
> Consider the situation of the scientist who performs experiments. Sometimes the experiments tried work, and that is just fine. But when exactly does the scientist learn most? Often, when an experiment flops. Such failures are the occasion to reflect on what went wrong and on what can one learn for the next time.
>
> Well, a similar process might occur in your own situation. Sometimes you can use coping efforts and they will work fine, but at other times they might fail. When will you learn most? Often when you say to yourself or to me, "It doesn't work." What exactly is the "It"? What did you try to do? "Doesn't work"—what does that mean? Do you have too high a standard for success? Do you expect too much? Recall the old adage "nothing ventured, nothing gained."

The trainer can use a variety of metaphors to convey the notion of inoculation to failure. SIT trainers have used such examples as comparing oneself to a sports coach who works collaboratively with athletes to analyze what can be improved for the competition. Or, another example is a coach teaching a new skill.

> I want you to think of me as a coach. For example, in teaching someone to ride a two-wheeled bicycle, I can begin by running alongside, holding onto the bike seat. As the rider begins to pick up speed, he says, "Okay, let go." As I let go, the rider might continue, but perhaps he falls. The fall is the occasion for us to find out what went wrong. Did he go too fast? Did he turn too quickly? Was the road too slippery? On such occasions, when we fall, often we learn the most. Similarly when you say, "It doesn't work," that is the occasion for us to learn most about coping with stress.

Three observations should be made about this technique of inoculation to failure. *First*, the clinical art in training is to find the right metaphor for each client, tailoring the specific examples to be offered, as well as their timing. *Second*, it is worth noting that the trainer is using a paradoxical approach of giving the client the license to fail. By inoculating the client to such failures, setbacks, backsliding, the trainer is attempting to defuse possible future negative emotions and thoughts. *Third*, the clinical ploy of using the client's expression "It did not work" lays the groundwork for explicitly teaching problem-solving skills.

PROBLEM-SOLVING TRAINING

As in the case of cognitive therapy, much has been written about the use of problem-solving training as a means of enhancing clients' coping skills[5] (e.g., D'Zurilla & Nezu, 1982; Goldfried & Davison, 1976; Sobel & Worden, 1981; Wasik, 1984). Common to each of these programs is a sequential problem-solving algorithm that includes these steps:

1. Define the stressor or stress reactions as a problem-to-be-solved,
2. Set realistic goals as concretely as possible by stating the problem in behavioral terms and by delineating steps necessary to reach each goal,
3. Generate a wide range of possible alternative courses of action,
4. Imagine and consider how others might respond if asked to deal with a similar stress problem,
5. Evaluate the pros and cons of each proposed solution and rank order the solutions from least to most practical and desirable,
6. Rehearse strategies and behaviors by means of imagery, behavioral rehearsal, and graduated practice,
7. Try out the most acceptable and feasible solution,
8. Expect some failures, but reward self for having tried,
9. Reconsider the original problem in light of the attempt at problem solving.

Wasik (1984) has translated each of the problem-solving steps into questions that one can ask oneself.

Steps	Questions/Actions
Problem identification	What is the concern?
Goal selection	What do I want?
Generation of alternatives	What can I do?
Consideration of consequences	What might happen?
Decision making	What is my decision?
Implementation	Now do it!
Evaluation	Did it work?

Wasik has also developed a problem-solving log whereby clients can identify a stressful problem and then try to answer each of the self-inter-

---

[5]Heppner, Neal, and Larsen (1984) have noted the potential use of problem-solving training as prevention with college students. They proposed that a number of high-risk groups could benefit from an SIT problem-solving approach including students on academic probation, students with a high potential for dropping out of university, adult women returning to school, students who were abused as children, recent divorcées and dual-career couples.

rogative probes. In addition to such self-query, the SIT trainer encourages clients to:

1. Talk to others in order to obtain relevant information,
2. Review how they have coped with past stressful events, with the objective of encouraging clients to recognize that potential coping skills probably already exist in their repertoires and that those coping skills might be transferable to the present stressful situation,
3. Chunk stressful events into smaller, more manageable tasks,
4. Make contingency plans for future eventualities, drawing an analogy to the game plans that sports teams make or the contingency plans that astronauts can follow,
5. Mentally rehearse ways of handling each mini-stress,
6. View any possible failures or disappointments as needed feedback to begin the problem-solving process once again.

A productive way to begin the problem-solving process is to ask clients what advice they would have for someone else who had a similar stressful experience? Or what advice might they offer themselves on a good day? Such queries encourage clients to appreciate that they often have problem-solving capacities within their repertoires and that one's thoughts and feelings can inhibit or interfere with their deployment. In this way the trainer can help clients reframe stressors as problems to be solved rather than as personal threats or provocations.

Two caveats need to be highlighted with regard to problem-solving training as a means of stress reduction. *First*, it is important to note that some clients are probably able to ''talk a good game'' in terms of problem solving, but they might not be able to translate such plans into effective action. Clients might specify that they should call upon others for help (i.e., mobilize social supports), but they might not know how to accomplish this objective, being unaware of how they inadvertently turn others off. Thus, there is a need for SIT trainers to ensure that clients have specific skills within their repertoires. The next chapter will consider the ways in which role-playing, modeling, imagery rehearsal, and graduated practice can be used to help clients implement and assess the outcome of their problem-solving plans. Many instrumental skills besides mobilizing social support could be needed to improve a person's coping abilities. These include competence in such areas as communicating, time management, setting priorities, and values clarification as well as specific coping skills that are applicable to specific populations (e.g., attention diversion techniques for pain patients).

The *second* warning concerns the very first step in the proposed problem-solving routine, namely, the identification of the problem. Sometimes the ostensible definition of a problem, even when stated in operationally be-havioral terms, is not enough because it is not the only problem that bears clinical attention. For example, Robin (1981) has developed a useful prob-lem-solving communication program for reducing parent-adolescent con-flict. Robin's program focuses on teaching the two parties (parents and adolescents) to identify and define problems and to negotiate solutions. A recent case illustrates some of the difficulties that can arise from pre-mature definition of the problem. Although the ostensible problem for the stressed family was the adolescent's curfew time, the major contributing factor was the family dynamic or family system—the mother felt trapped in the home and envied the daughter's freedom. This led to the mother's harassing the father to do something about the adolescent's so-called "libertine attitude." Focusing on negotiation skills between the parents and the adolescent was helpful, but another important aspect of SIT train-ing was the need to attend to the mother's unexpressed current concerns about her lack of control, which she imposed on many family conflicts. The SIT trainer was able to work with the family to consider the common-alities or themes that cut across the various family stressful situations. The point quite simply is that the premature definition of a problem based on observables can prove too limiting in understanding and treating stressful events.

This is *not* a call for long-term, in-depth, dynamically oriented family therapy, nor for a search for so-called "deeper problems" in all instances of stressed populations. Instead, this is a call for SIT trainers to be sen-sitive to the underlying meaning that interpersonal conflicts can hold for clients and significant others.

SELF-INSTRUCTIONAL TRAINING, OR GUIDED SELF-DIALOGUE

If you examine treatment manuals on SIT you will notice a section that lists possible self-statements that stressed clients can say to themselves while preparing for a stressor, when confronting and handling a stressful event, when feeling overwhelmed with stress, and, finally, when reflect-ing on their coping efforts. These four phases correspond to the various stages offered in the reconceptualization process. What function do such self-statements serve, and how does the SIT trainer prepare clients for and enlist their cooperation in the use of such self-statements?

Self-instructional training is designed to nurture a problem-solving at-titude and to engender specific cognitive strategies that clients can use at various phases of their stress response. More specifically, the guided self-dialogue is designed to help clients to:

1. assess the demands of a situation and plan for future stressors,
2. control negative self-defeating, stress-engendering thoughts, images, and feelings,
3. acknowledge, use, and relabel the arousal experienced,
4. cope with intense dysfunctional emotions that might be experienced,
5. "psych" themselves up to confront stressful situations, and
6. reflect on their performance and reinforce themselves for having attempted to cope.

To achieve these objectives, the trainer begins by reviewing with clients the various stages of their stress experience. For example, the trainer can state:

> Before, we were discussing the situations in which you become distressed, for instance, the daily hassles that set you off. (Trainer gives several examples.) We commented on how one can view your stress reactions as going through various stages. (Both trainer and client offer examples of the four stages—preparation for stressor, confrontation, critical moments, and self-reflection.) In each of these four phases, what you think and feel plays a key role in influencing your stress reaction. (Once again the trainer and the client offer several examples from the client's account that illustrate the important role of the appraisal process on the client's stress reactions.)
>
> In fact, the way we think can affect how we feel in a fairly direct, intentional fashion. We each influence our thoughts by a sort of *internal monologue*—an ongoing series of *statements to ourselves*—in which we tell ourselves what to think and believe and even how to behave.
>
> You might find that speaking about your thoughts as "self-statements" is somewhat unexpected. But there is good reason for using this phrase. Calling a thought a "statement to yourself" emphasizes the deliberateness of that particular thought, and the fact that it is under your control. Let's consider the kinds of thoughts or self-statements and images you had before, during, and after your stress reaction.

The discussion of the client's stressful experience provides the basis for the development of coping self-statements. If the client's thoughts can make stress worse, then it is not a big step for the client to suggest that different thoughts (self-statements) can be employed at each phase to reduce, avoid, or constructively use stress. In a collaborative manner, the trainer and the client consider possible coping self-statements.

Table 5.2 provides an illustrative list of self-statements that have been used in SIT and the purposes they are designed to serve. Specific coping self-statements are tailored to the needs of each population. Clients are also encouraged to translate the self-statements into their own words and to personalize them in a meaningful manner. The self-statements should not be too general, for that might lead to rote repetition. Self-statements that relate to competence and control seem to work best. For instance, those self-statements are quite helpful that assist the client in focusing on the present, trying to take things as they come rather than considering negative future consequences (e.g., "What if something terrible happens?"). Similarly, self-statements that direct specific thoughts, emotions, and behaviors are also useful, as noted by one client.

> It (self-instructing) makes me able to be in the situation, not to be comfortable, but to tolerate it . . . I don't talk myself out of being afraid, just out of appearing afraid . . . You immediately react to the thing you're afraid of and then start to reason with yourself. I talk myself out of panic.

Following several such successful attempts, she reported that even the feeling of being afraid dissipated, and she no longer appraised the situation as stressful.

Altmaier et al. (1982) have developed an interesting technique to foster the use of self-statements. Her clients establish a contract with themselves by completing the following incomplete sentences:

> In order to cope more successfully, I will pause when I notice my stress signals of_____.
> I will examine my feelings, images, self-statements such as_____.
> If I am using negative self-talk, I will switch to telling myself_____.
> I will relax myself by_____.
> I will reward myself for having used my self-talk by means of_____.

She also has clients use a mnemonic device (STIRR) to remember the coping sequence, namely,

> *S*ense stress when it first occurs
> *T*hink about my self-talk
> *I*nstruct self to replace negative coping thoughts and
>   feelings
> *R*elax self actively
> *R*eward self for having tried to cope

Many variations of Altmaier's contract and mnemonic approach have been offered (see Turk et al., 1983). The important caveat is to ensure that the client does not view the mnemonic as a rigid formula, believing that the coping responses subsumed in the mnemonic are the only ones to be employed. In most instances, I have shied away from using such mnemonics because they often convey a too-simplistic formula-based view of the coping process. However, with the proper precautions they can prove helpful.

In perusing the cognitive strategies listed in Table 5.2, it is important to appreciate that they are not offered as catchphrases or verbal palliatives

Table 5.2. Examples of Coping Self-statements Used in Stress Inoculation Training

---

Preparing For Stressor

Purpose   Focus on specific preparation for task
Combat negative thinking
Emphasize planning and preparation

Examples What do I have to do?
I can develop a plan to deal with it.
Just think about what I can do about it.
This could be a rough situation.
I can work out a plan to handle this.
Remember, stick to the issues and don't take it personally.
Stop worrying. Worrying won't help anything.
What are some of the helpful things I can do instead?
I'm feeling uptight—that's natural.
Maybe I'm just eager to confront the situation.

Confronting and Handling Stressor

Purpose   Control stress reaction
Reassure that one can handle situation
Reinterpret stress as something that can be used constructively
Reminder to use coping responses such as relaxation
Remain focused on task or situation

Examples Just "psych" yourself up—I can meet this challenge.
I can convince myself to do it.
One step at a time.
Just chunk the stress into manageable units.
Don't think about my stress, just about what I have to do.
This stress is what the trainer said I might feel.
It is a reminder to use my coping exercises.
This tenseness can be an ally, a cue to cope.
Relax, I'm in control. Take a slow deep breath. Ah, good.
As long as I keep my cool, I'm in control of the situation.
Don't make more out of this than I have to.
Look for positives, don't jump to conclusions.
I have a lot of different coping techniques I can call upon.
Things are not as serious as I make them out to be.
I can just sit back and take it easy.

(continued)

to be repeated mindlessly. There is a difference between the SIT use of problem-solving strategies and the use of a "psychological litany" or formula that tends to lead to rote repetition and emotionless patter. The trainer does not suggest, "here is a list of things to say to yourself that will make stress go away." One should *not* equate the guided self-dialogue with the power-of-positive-thinking approach espoused by Norman Vincent Peale and W. Clement Stone. Although there is an element of positive thinking and self-reliance inherent in the self-instructional training, there is still a difference between providing clients with a questionable verbal

Table 5.2. (*continued*)

Coping with Feelings of Being Overwhelmed
Purpose   This stage does *not* always occur
          Set up contingency plans, prepare for possibility of becoming extremely stressed
          Prepare to deal with worst situation when feeling out of control and overwhelmed
          Encourage to remain in situation
          Stay focused on present
          Accept feelings and wait for them to decrease
          Learn to have some control even if worst happens
Examples When stress comes, just pause.
          Keep my focus on the present; what is it I have to do?
          Label my stress on a 0 to 10 scale and watch it change.
          I should expect my stress to rise sometimes.
          Don't try to eliminate stress totally; just keep it manageable.
          My muscles are getting tight.
          Relax and slow things down.
          Time to take a slow deep breath.
          Let's take the issue point by point.
          My stress is a signal.
          Time for problem solving.

Evaluation of Coping Efforts and Self-Rewards
Purpose   Evaluate attempt, what helped and what didn't
          Look back over experience to see what has been learned
          Recognize small gains, don't belittle gradual progress
          Praise self for trying
          Keep trying, don't expect perfection
          What you would have done differently or better
Examples It wasn't as bad as I expected.
          I made more out of stress than it was worth.
          It's getting better each time I use this procedure.
          It didn't work. That's okay.
          What can I learn from my try.
          I can be pleased with the progress I'm making.
          Wait until I tell the others how it went.
          I handled it pretty well.
          Good, I did it. Next time I'll do even better.

palliative and the active problem-solving training that is being proposed here. The rejection of schools of positive thinking as being too simpleminded should not lead trainers to neglect how cognitive control can be employed to help clients cope with stress more effectively.

The trainer does not present the list of self-statements to the client as a fait accompli, nor convey to the client that these are statements that should be memorized and said in a rote fashion whenever he or she feels stressed, as in the tradition of Emil Coué (the French psychiatrist), who enjoined his clients to say, "Every day, in every way, I'm getting better and better." Instead, the SIT trainer works with the client in a collaborative fashion to generate a meaningful list of cognitive strategies. For example, the trainer can state:

> In the last session we discussed some of the thoughts and feelings you have in stressful situations and some of the alternative self-statements you might employ at each phase of your stressful reaction. I thought it might be useful if I summarized our discussion. So, I have taken the liberty of putting together a list of self-statements that you can use before, during, and after stressful events. I have included your suggestions and some suggestions that other clients like yourself have offered as being helpful.
>
> What I would like us to do is to take a few minutes to look over this list and then to discuss them. In reviewing this list of coping self-statements, keep in mind that each person's situation is slightly different and that each of you is unique. Look over the list with an eye to deciding what might be worth considering in your case.

At this point, the client considers the coping self-statements and how and when they could be of use. For example, how one can neutralize negative self-statements by using them as cues for the production of coping self-statements. In this way treatment generalization is built into the intervention. The client's own stressful reactions provide the built-in reminder to select and use one's coping response. The trainer should also query the client on how he or she feels about the idea of self-talk (e.g., "something only crazy people do"), in order to convey the important role private speech plays in self-regulation.

In summary, self-instructional training begins by identifying the client's habitual self-statements, images, and feelings that occur during various phases of stressful experiences. The client and the trainer then consider how these self-statements might exacerbate the stress reaction and interfere with performance of adaptive coping responses. Next, they collaborate in the generation of alternative self-statements that signal the production of more adaptive coping responses. The client is encouraged to personalize these self-statements by using her or his own words in developing coping strategies. The list of coping self-statements can be adapted and extended as the training continues.

ROLE OF DENIAL

The discussion of the cognitive interventions (cognitive therapy, problem solving, and self-instructional training) highlights the role of testing the validity of one's thoughts and feelings. In some stressful situations, however, such active mental and behavioral coping responses might not be stress-reducing. There are some instances where doing nothing, not thinking about stressful events, can be a more adaptive coping response. Lazarus (1984) has written thoughtfully about the adaptive value of denial, especially in circumstances in which it is impossible to exert control. Although the psychoanalytic model postulates that denial involves an unconscious defensive distortion that is not under voluntary control, from a transactional perspective the tolerance and even the nurturance of denial can be a useful training strategy. Denial can act as a means of self-protection, facilitating gradual exposure to a stressor. Denial can be a way to pace oneself, handling only so much stress at one time and slowly increasing exposure as one gradually assimilates the meaning of the information. Insisting that clients must face the reality of their situations or express their feelings can be potentially harmful.

When doing nothing won't make a difference to the outcome, then clients have little to lose from not attending to their stress. In such situations, denial in the form of maintaining detachment, rationalization, or even self-deception can help individuals to feel better, to maintain feelings of hope and a sense of self-worth. As Lazarus noted, denial can serve the constructive value of helping individuals not to become overwhelmed and providing them with the time needed to marshal other coping resources. However, in some instances, denial can be maladaptive when it retards necessary direct action modes of coping.

The SIT trainer needs to consider that, under certain stressful conditions, denial can represent a useful means of coping. The trainer could even remind clients of the observation attributed to Reinhold Niebuhr (later adopted as a motto by Alcoholics Anonymous), "God, grant me the strength to change what I can, the courage to tolerate what I cannot, and the wisdom to know the difference." The lesson for the trainer is to be cautious about imposing his or her set of values or one set of coping procedures as the norm. A key feature of any stress management program is to help clients appreciate when to appraise situations as uncontrollable, in order to select the appropriate coping process. In some instances the best coping process is to abandon efforts directed at altering the situation. There is a clear need to individually tailor or customize the training to both the demands of the situation and the capabilities of the client.

SUMMARY

The major objective of the second phase of SIT training is to help clients develop and consolidate a variety of intrapersonal and interpersonal coping skills. The coping skills that are trained emerge naturally from the reconceptualization process. The specific training techniques reviewed included relaxation training, cognitive restructuring procedures, problem solving, and self-instructional training. The chapter concluded with emphasis on the need to individually tailor interventions because in some instances denial can be a more adaptive coping response than the more validity oriented cognitive approaches. Clinical guidelines needed to implement these training procedures were reviewed.

Chapter 6
Application and Follow-Through Phase

The focus of the training thus far has been on helping clients change their view of stress and develop coping skills. The objectives of the third phase of SIT training are to encourage clients to implement coping responses in day-to-day situations and to maximize chances of generalized change. The trainer uses paced mastery, in which small manageable units of stress are induced in vitro and gradually in vivo. SIT trainers do not leave the transfer to chance nor do they expect that coping skills that were practiced in the clinic will automatically generalize to the "real world." The client's old well-established response habits and expectations must be overcome.

To achieve these goals, the trainer can employ a variety of techniques including imagery and behavioral rehearsal, role-playing, modeling, and graduated in vivo practice. The specific techniques can be tailored to the needs of each population. We will consider each of these procedures and conclude with a consideration of how one prepares clients for posttraining experiences.

IMAGERY REHEARSAL

Imagery has been used in two major ways in SIT. It has been employed as a specific means of attention diversion with pain patients and other stressed populations (see McCaffery, 1979; Meichenbaum, 1978; Turk et al., 1983). The other major way it has been used is to provide clients with an opportunity to rehearse coping skills or to engage in what is known as the "work of worrying" (Breznitz, 1971; Janis, 1958; Marmor, 1958). By means of imagery or role playing, the client can rehearse coping efforts in the training sessions that approximate the stressful situation. Subsequent in vivo practice can then be planned, implemented, and evaluated.

The general format for the imagery rehearsal procedure is derived from Wolpe's (1959) systematic desensitization paradigm. The client and the trainer collaboratively generate a hierarchy of scenes, from least to most stressful. The various stressful scenes can be ascertained from the client's self-monitoring exercises (e.g., stress-log and automatic thoughts records), interviews, and so forth. It is often quite educational and therapeutic to discuss with clients the dimensions underlying various stressful situations and to hierarchically arrange them.

As in desensitization, the client is asked to imagine coping with progressively more threatening scenes while relaxed. However, instead of following Wolpe's practice of terminating the scene when the client experiences stress, in SIT the client is asked to imagine coping with the stressful situation. The scenes highlight low-intensity intrapersonal and interpersonal cues that signal the onset of a stressful situation or a stressful reaction. The goal is to have clients learn to notice, even anticipate, signs of distress, so they can become cues that produce coping responses. To maximize the similarity between imagery rehearsal and real-life experiences, *coping* imagery is employed. Coping imagery[1] involves clients imagining themselves becoming stressed, having stress-engendering thoughts and feelings, and then coping with these difficulties using the coping skills they have acquired. The clients' images can provide some of the same functions as a model. In this way, daily hassles or stressful life events can be viewed as opportunities to practice one's coping skills. For example, if we go back to the incident of putting my four children to bed, the trainer could say:

> Don, now that we have worked on various ways in which you can cope with stress and the ways in which these daily hassles vary in intensity, let us practice how you can use your coping resources. As we did last week, I will ask you to imagine various stressful situations and the ways in which you are able to cope with them. Let's begin the imagery with the scene of putting your children to bed. Sitting back in the chair, relaxed, conjure up the scene. . . .

At this point the trainer helps the client visualize the scene as clearly and vividly as possible, as if the client is there noting details and sensory experience, and encouraging the client to reexperience any thoughts and feelings he or she would have in that situation. Usually, the scene lasts for 1 to 5 minutes in length. For instance:

> Don, imagine that you are cleaning up after dinner. All of a sudden you hear a sound from the bathroom. . . . What is it? On no, no, not David running in the tub again. How many times have I told him? You can feel the tenseness building in your arms, your breathing becomes heavier (trainer uses the client's stress symptoms). As you begin to barrel up the stairs, you are

[1]Kazdin (1973), Meichenbaum (1971), and Sarason (1975) have provided evidence of the therapeutic value of coping over mastery modeling and imagery. Mastery imagery involves clients viewing themselves as being only successful in handling stressful transactions.

able to pause just for a moment, take a slow deep breath, and, as you exhale
slowly, you are able to gain your composure as you climb the stairs. See yourself coping with your stress. . . . Relax. . . . Good.

The client is encouraged to use any personally generated self-statements
and images that would facilitate coping. As in the desensitization procedure, if clients experience difficulty in reducing stress for any one scene,
the trainer can go back to a less intensely stressful scene from the hierarchy. Turk et al. (1983, pp. 321–327) describe the imagery rehearsal procedure in more detail.

This example illustrates that the trainer includes images of high probability stressful events that the client is likely to encounter, specific low-
intensity intrapersonal and interpersonal cues, and examples of how the
client notices, interrupts, and copes with his or her stress. The trainer
could even include intense stressful reactions, as when the client becomes
overwhelmed, "catastrophizing," doubting his or her ability to cope. The
image continues as the client notices and interrupts such negative stress-
engendering thoughts and feelings. In short, the trainer tries to anticipate
and subsume future stressful transactions into the imagery rehearsal. The
trainer can also include mastery images, where the client successfully
copes, and coping images. Such imagery rehearsal can help the client
identify potential roadblocks and gain distance, or objectify, stressful
events. In this way, the client's stressful reactions take on a dejà vu
flavor, acting as cues to use one's coping responses.

Throughout the imagery rehearsal procedure, there is a need to check
with clients about their reactions to the imagery process, discussing their
ability to visualize and how and when they can use coping techniques in
vivo. This latter point needs to be underscored. The trainer should *not* take
for granted that clients will spontaneously see the applicability or autonomously generalize the coping routine beyond the training session. There
is a need to have the client rephrase in his or her own words why and
how using the imagery rehearsal procedure will help him or her cope more
effectively with stress.

BEHAVIORAL REHEARSAL,
ROLE-PLAYING, AND MODELING

Closely related to the imagery rehearsal procedure is behavioral rehearsal. As noted, there is a need to ensure that the client is able to practice
and demonstrate behavioral skills in the training session. The coping skills
vary, depending upon the specific population. These can include communication skills, mobilizing social supports, and anger control. The general
format for this aspect of SIT is for the client and the trainer to anticipate
stressful interactions and to behaviorally rehearse ways of coping. The

trainer and the client can periodically exchange roles, so that the trainer can model specific coping responses. An example of this approach was offered by West, Horan, and Games (1984) in their SIT of nurses. The nurses were exposed to eight common stress-producing situations via role-playing, in order to practice handling stress. The scenarios were derived from the nursing literature and from the participants' experiences. For example, one scene involved the following scenario:

> Your supervisor calls you into her office and states that she needs an inventory completed on supplies by the end of the shift. Two patients have continually been pressing the call button. The telephone calls just won't stop. You had to leave three patients to change sheets, complete rounds with the physician, and chart orders. You had to verbally reprimand an orderly for smoking in a patient's room. Everybody has been coming to you for answers on new procedures just instituted. You just can't find the time to complete an employee evaluation and get the inventory report completed as requested. You've been running all morning with no break in your schedule. Your muscles feel tight and you've got one hell of a headache.

Some SIT trainers have used modeling films of particular coping responses. The coping modeling films use a voice overplay, where several models not only behaviorally demonstrate becoming stressed and coping, but also voice their thoughts and feelings. This is achieved by telling the client that the trainer has taken films of other clients like them and that they were asked to share their feelings and thoughts, which are included on the tape. By using a coping modeling film, the trainer can anticipate and subsume the high probability thoughts and feelings a client is likely to experience. Such modeling films should be followed by the trainer and the client's discussing their reactions to the film and what they can learn from other people's coping efforts. Such discussion is followed by the client's rehearsing, receiving feedback, fine-tuning his or her coping repertoire. Such feedback training is often quite useful when SIT is conducted on a group basis.

Another way to accomplish skills training is to ask the client to role-play the trainer while the trainer assumes the role of a "novice client." The task is for the client to coach the novice client on how to cope effectively. The attitude-change literature suggests that such an approach helps to promote change, as the client is likely to generate strategies, arguments, examples, and motivating appeals that are most personally convincing (Janis & Mann, 1977). This type of role-playing also provides an opportunity to assess the client's understanding of the training strategies. The next chapter considers the ways in which stress scripts have been used in SIT with various populations.

Examples of where such behavioral rehearsal and role-playing exercises have been used include:

1. Coping with experimentally induced pain by pain patients (Turk et al., 1983)
2. Coping with anger control in police officers and adolescent offenders (Feindler & Fremouw, 1983; Novaco, 1977b; Sarason et al., 1979)
3. Seeking help from others (Wasik, 1984)
4. Being assertive with one's physician (Sobel & Worden, 1981)
5. Resolving conflicts between adolescents and parents (Robin, 1981)
6. Handling job-related stress by nurses (West et al., 1984)

No matter what the population, the major guideline emphasized is the need for flexibility. Coping responses that work at one time can prove ineffective in another situation or at another time. In fact, clients are encouraged to anticipate high-risk failure situations and to plan ahead for such occasions. Such preplanning lowers the risk of clients becoming overwhelmed at the time of most severe stress. Clients are reminded that no category or type of coping strategy has proven to be universally effective and that the object of the training is to provide them with a description of and training in the use of a number of coping strategies, so they can pick and choose and experiment in determining what works best for them.

Bandura's (1977) work on self-efficacy theory suggests that the generalization of such coping skills occurs most readily under conditions where the client feels that the required behaviors can be produced (efficacy expectations) and that the desired outcome will occur when the response is adequately produced (outcome expectations). These expectations occur when the trainer can arrange for the client to employ the coping response (a) in vivo, (b) under circumstances where there is a high probability that the response will produce the desired outcome, and (c) under conditions that allow the client to attribute success to personal capability or paced mastery rather than to external factors. A number of techniques can be used to consolidate the effects of SIT including modeling, joint performance with the trainer, and graduated in vivo exposure.

GRADUATED IN VIVO EXPOSURE

The literature on stress management indicates that, the closer the training sessions are to the criterion situation, the greater the generalization. Moreover, whenever possible, the client is encouraged to rehearse in vivo in the form of graded homework assignments. The homework assignments that clients undertake should be concrete, observable, and measurable, and they should increase in difficulty over the course of training. As Shelton and Ackerman (1974) noted, homework assignments should include a *do* statement and a *quantity* statement indicating what the client will accomplish and how often the tasks are to be completed, respectively.

There is a need to ensure that the homework assignments are realistic and relevant. In fact, the trainer needs to lay the groundwork for clients so that they may collaborate in generating the homework assignments. The trainer should ask clients what suggestions they have for trying out their coping skills. In short, it is more likely clients will undertake homework assignments if they have suggested them. There is a need to tap the clients' views about conducting each exercise.

In order to avoid any misunderstandings, clients could be asked to write down the homework assignments they agree to complete. A careful comprehension check is conducted, and any possible difficulties are considered.

The trainer should conscientiously check with clients on the outcome of the homework assignments, conveying the importance assigned to such efforts. If clients fail to do a homework assignment, the trainer needs to consider in a collaborative manner the reasons for such failure. Was the cause a misunderstanding, a memory failure, an unsupportive environment, excessive demands, fear of failure, fear of succeeding, or some form of resistance? Often it is useful to characterize homework assignments as "personal experiments" whereby clients can find out what works and what still needs to be done.

The trainer needs to ensure that clients set only modest goals, sometimes involving small steps. Demands should be increased only following several successes. To ensure that clients make self-attributions, the trainer should adopt a Columbo-stance, analyzing with them how they did in fact handle the stressful situation and accomplish success, for instance,

> You say you actually were able to handle that stressful event. What exactly happened? . . . How did you pull it off? . . . You really were able to get them to help you in that situation.
>
> How would you compare yourself now to when you first came in? . . . In what ways have you changed? . . . It sounds to me, and correct me if I am wrong, that you have been able to bring about important changes.

If failures are reported, it is important to explore the client's criterion of success: clients can misread partial successes (often the best that can be realistically expected) as unmitigated failure. There is also a need to explore how the client coped with failure and what was learned from it.

Rehearsal of homework exercises in the session and careful attention to clients' evaluations of their likelihood of success can also help clients avoid failure experience. Sometimes the homework assignment can be conducted in vivo under the trainer's guidance. Three examples will illustrate this possibility. Wernick (1983) used SIT with burn patients and had them use coping skills under trainer guidance while undergoing tanking (painful bathing).

The second example comes from my own clinical experience, where psychiatric inpatients and adolescent retardates, as well as their counselors (frontline staff), were taught coping skills. Joint stress management sessions were conducted with both client and counselors. Both in sessions and on the ward, counselors modeled how they used the coping skills to control their own stress, and they could prompt and guide clients in the use of the coping procedures. In fact, clients would remind counselors when they should use coping strategies such as relaxation and problem solving. Counselors and clients had rap sessions at the end of the day to review how they used their coping skills and to consider when they could use such skills the next day (i.e., identification of high-risk situations). The basic idea was to build generalization into the day-to-day transactions.

The third example comes from the work of Fremouw and Harmatz (1975), who found that stressed clients who acted as helpers and taught stress reduction procedures to other stressed clients showed more improvement than those who only learned the stress coping techniques. Putting clients in the role of helper could represent another important application opportunity.

RELAPSE PREVENTION

Special mention should be made of the important concept of relapse prevention in SIT. Marlatt and Gordon (1984) have developed a treatment approach for working with alcoholics, drug addicts, and smokers. A central feature of their training is to help patients learn to identify and successfully deal with factors that could contribute to relapse. For example, in the case of alcoholics, the focus is on high-risk situations where they are tempted to drink and on the specific behavioral and cognitive skills needed to cope with such temptations. The training is designed to anticipate and subsume the reactions clients are likely to have when they violate abstinence and teach them how they can plan coping activities before such stressors occur. The work with addictions indicates that the name of the game is not to have clients stop per se, but instead to have them stay off the addictive substance. Moreover, if clients do backslide, the goal of relapse prevention training is to ensure that they don't go back to their old base rate level. The focus of training shifts to the clients' reactions when they violate abstinence, for example, "Once an alcoholic, always an alcoholic," "Look, we are all going to die anyway, pass me a cigarette," "I knew this program wouldn't work for me. What's the use?"

The concept of relapse prevention is as relevant to the field of stress management as it is to the treatment of addictions. In both instances, the way clients interpret a slip, failure, or relapse is critical. If the client interprets the slip as evidence of inadequate personal efficacy, this appraisal can undermine subsequent coping efforts. The client might infer that he or she is not really capable of handling stressors and give up. To reduce this risk, SIT trainers encourage clients to anticipate failures and setbacks and have them rehearse how they will respond to such lapses. Marlatt and Gordon have even suggested that treatment include planned failure experiences ("programmed relapse"), to develop appropriate coping responses and to establish a sense of self-efficacy in the face of such slips. Trainers can use spontaneous relapses that occur during the course of training as opportunities to develop resilience (i.e., a sense of confidence that one can "get back on track" after setbacks).

The discussion of relapse, however, must be done in a delicate fashion. On the one hand, the trainer does not wish to convey an expectancy that training will inevitably lead to failure, but on the other hand, the trainer wishes to anticipate and subsume into training clients' possible reactions to the likely recurrence of stress. One possible way of dealing with such relapse is for the trainer to reanalyze with the client previous reactions that have followed relapses. The trainer can also use imaginary other clients, noting their reactions to failure and how they coped with such outcomes. The trainer can then ask clients if they are likely to have such feelings and thoughts.

Because stress is a normal part of life, clients should recognize that they will continue to experience it even after successful training. The goal of SIT is not to eliminate stress but to learn to respond adaptively in stressful situations and to be resilient in the face of failure.

FOLLOW-THROUGH

The last phase of SIT is concerned with follow-through, or the extension of the training into the future. The client and the trainer should *not* consider the training program as ending per se, but rather as switching into a different phase. In most SIT programs, some form of follow-up or booster sessions has been built into the training regimen. The timing of such sessions has varied with the specific population and the exigencies of the situation. The training is usually faded, with the last sessions being every 2 weeks instead of weekly. In this way, the training is not terminated abruptly, but instead sessions are thinned out during a transitional period.

Follow-up and booster sessions can take place at 3-, 6-, and 12-month periods, as an incentive for patients and to fine-tune coping skills and troubleshoot about any client difficulties. The frequency and timing of such follow-up sessions varies from case to case. At this point, there are little or no data about the most effective timing or manner of such post-training contacts.

The trainer also conveys to clients that the "door is always open" in case of any difficulties. Just signifying the availability of such help could be sufficient to nurture coping skills. Initiating such contact should be construed as an adaptive coping response.

In considering the use of booster sessions, it is important to remember that the nature of the client's problems can change over time. With client improvement, there could also be changes in the expectations by significant others. The stressful events that brought clients to training are unlikely to be the same as those that clients deal with at follow-up.

It is also important to have posttraining plans defined and agreed upon. As part of these plans, the trainer and the client should explore how the client will determine if further help is needed. For example, Karol, Doerfler, Parker, and Armentraut (1981) provided stressed medical patients with a checklist of questions to consider when deciding to use the health care system (see Turk et al., 1983, p. 337). A similar checklist could be developed for other stressed populations. The goal is to educate clients about the pros and cons of seeking additional help.

A review with clients of what they have learned from training and how they have changed from the pretraining phase can contribute to feelings of self-efficacy and competence. Clients can discuss current and anticipated life events that might be problematic and stressful. The object is to help clients realize that they have plans and abilities to cope with stressful events. Such discussion conveys the trainer's expectation and conviction that the changes that have been achieved will be maintained and will probably even grow.

Finally, in some settings such as working with stressed occupational groups (police officers, teachers, athletes), the SIT can be extended beyond initial training and be included as part of the on-the-job experience. In the next chapter, we will explore the many opportunities for building stress management programs into work settings. Instead of SIT being a one-shot, limited intervention, it is fascinating to project the use of such principles as part of an ongoing stress reduction program.

SUMMARY

The major objective of the third phase of SIT is to help clients practice their coping skills both in the training sessions and in vivo. Such techniques as imagery and behavioral rehearsal, modeling, role-playing, and graduated in vivo practice were reviewed. Clinical guidelines for the intervention for each procedure were considered. The importance of the concept of relapse prevention for fostering feelings of self-efficacy and resilience was reviewed. SIT training can be extended into the future by the use of booster sessions and follow-up and follow-through interventions.

Chapter 7
Specific Applications of Stress Inoculation Training

As noted in chapter 3, SIT has been applied to a number of diverse populations on both a treatment and a prevention basis. In this chapter, we will describe several examples of how SIT has been applied to specific populations. References indicate where more detailed accounts can be obtained.

APPLYING SIT IN MEDICAL SETTINGS

In recent years, a major area for psychologically based interventions has been medical settings, as reflected in the emerging fields of behavioral medicine and health psychology. The application of SIT in behavioral medicine has been reviewed by Turk, Meichenbaum, and Genest (1983). They have offered a very detailed treatment manual of SIT with acute and chronic pain patients. They also described how SIT has been applied to a host of patients who suffer from a variety of medical problems (e.g., headaches, dysmennorrhea, cancer, backaches, arthritis, and burns).

Another major medical population to whom SIT has been applied is patients preparing for surgery and medical and dental examinations. A number of psychological techniques have been used to teach medical patients coping strategies in order to reduce their preprocedural and preoperational anxiety and fear and their postoperative pain and suffering. The techniques include providing patients with information, counseling, modeling, behavioral and cognitive-behavioral interventions, and hypnosis. Anderson and Masur (1983) and MacDonald and Kuiper (1983) have reviewed the methodological limitations of these intervention studies.

Illustrative of SIT interventions with medical patients are the studies by Kendall, Williams, Pechacek, Graham, and Sisslak (1979), Langer et al. (1975), and Melamed and Siegel (1975). For example, in the last study, hospitalized children who viewed a film depicting a peer coping with surgery demonstrated better preoperative and postoperative adjustment on a variety of measures than did control groups. Interestingly, subsequent studies have suggested that coping models appear to be more effective than mastery or fearless models in reducing medically related anxiety (Anderson & Masur, 1983).

Langer et al. (1975) demonstrated a similar effect with adult surgery patients. They trained surgical patients to exercise cognitive control through selective attention, in order to distract themselves from negative aspects of surgery. The coping treatment involved the training of cognitive reappraisal techniques such as positive evaluations and calming self-statements. The surgery patients were told that often people are somewhat anxious before an operation, but that they could control their emotions if they knew how. It was explained that it is how people view events and the attention they give to these views, not the events themselves, that cause stress. Consistent with these introductory remarks, patients were given several examples from everyday life of alternative ways of viewing negative events, including undergoing surgery. Patients were asked to rehearse realistic, positive aspects of the surgical experience. Such training resulted in significant reductions in postsurgical distress, as reflected in nurses' observations and requests for sedatives as well as length of hospital stay.

Closely related to the Langer et al. intervention is the SIT procedure used by Kendall and his colleagues to prepare patients for cardiac catherization (see Kendall, 1983). Their preventative program included pretreatment contact and presentation of the rationale of the program, followed by information concerning sensory, procedural, and coping response information. The latter was offered in the form of a self-disclosing coping model. Such preliminary contacts provided the groundwork for the discussion and training of specific coping techniques such as relaxation, cognitive restructuring, and imaginal rehearsal. The training was tailored to the patient's particular coping style. Various potential internal and external stress cues were identified, so they could be used as signals to patients to employ their coping repertoires.

Such patient-oriented interventions can be (and should be) supplemented with systems-level interventions directed at medical staff (nurses, doctors, lab technicians). Volicer and Bohannon (1975) have developed a hospital stress rating scale that provides an extensive list of hospital-related stress experiences. Any stress reduction intervention in a medical setting should be consistent with the transactional perspective, not only focusing on teaching patients coping skills, but also considering how administrative policies and interpersonal styles of communicating can be altered to reduce and avoid stress. The data from such SIT interventions indicate that not only are patient suffering and distress reduced, but there is also a substantial financial savings. The preliminary studies indicate that it is good business as well as good therapy to undertake SIT interventions in medical settings.

Closely related to the issue of applying SIT to medical patients are recent efforts to provide stress management training to medical staff. Especially with the recent popularity of the concept of job burnout, a prime target for such intervention has been nurses. West et al. (1984) have recently summarized the nature of stress that nurses experience under four headings: Retrograde complaints involving bodily and psychological concerns; Assertiveness deficits reflecting interpersonal conflicts; Competency concerns involving task demands, given an exploding technology; and Time stress (summarized as ReACT). A stress inoculation training regimen was employed to encourage registered nurses to instrumentally alter environmental stressors and/or change their stress-engendering perceptions and reactions. SIT treatment was administered by a counselor, individually, twice a week, for 60 minutes, over a 4-week period. The training covered such topics as the nature of stress, self-monitoring of stress-producing events, and several coping skills (relaxation training, assertive skills building, cognitive restructuring, and time management instruction). Practice in handling stress was accomplished by means of role-playing with the counselor. The specific role-playing scenarios were chosen from the nursing literature and from the authors' experience in working with nurses. The program was found to be effective in reducing the nature of the stress experience. Such programs can readily be administered on a group basis.

APPLICATIONS TO SPECIFIC OCCUPATIONAL GROUPS

A number of occupational groups besides nurses work under conditions of high stress. One such group that has received a great deal of clinical attention is police officers. Illustrative of the application of SIT efforts to police officers are the programs developed by Sarason, Johnson, Berberich, and Siegel (1979) and Novaco (1977b). In Sarason's colleagues' program, they provided police academy trainees with six 2-hour training sessions. The training included instruction and practice in self-monitoring reactions to anger-provoking and threatening situations. This self-awareness was accomplished through role-playing, modeling, and self-monitoring of responses during stressful situations. Emphasis was on using cues in stressful situations as signals for the development of coping responses (relaxation, coping self-statements, and interpersonal skills). Trainees observed models who displayed adaptive coping responses in the face of stress, and then they practiced using coping skills under similar conditions. The training was effective in enhancing the trainees' coping skills, as judged by police academy personnel ratings on stressful mock scenes and on self-report measures. This was particularly evident when the training tasks closely approximated the specific situations likely to be encountered by the trainees. For example, Sarason et al. included role-playing scenes such as a policeman having to handle a suicidal woman, individuals involved in a landlord-tenant dispute, and two belligerent individuals involved in a traffic accident.

Novaco (1977b) also demonstrated the value of role-playing following coping skills training (e.g., actors were hired to act out provocative situations such as taunting and teasing police officers). Such behavioral rehearsal is followed by discussion of the participants' feelings and thoughts that occurred during the role-playing and how stress management skills were used. Any difficulties are enumerated, discussed, and rehearsed. As noted in the clinical guidelines in chapter 3, insofar as the trainer can make the training situations similar to the criterion situations, the likelihood of generalization is increased. The effectiveness of such prejob interventions or simulated job experiences is probably enhanced by continuing such programs when individuals actually are on the job.

Sarason et al. also underscored the need for trainers to be sensitive to participants' attitudes toward the training program. Some participants felt that taking stress management training was a "sign of weakness," because dealing with stress is supposed to "come naturally" and such training is considered unnecessary. This observation highlights the need to assess the participants' expectations and views about the training. Such training might be more appropriate for regular police officers or for volunteers. Another possibility is to arrange for the SIT training to be conducted by another police officer instead of by a "university-type" instructor.

Recent articles by Alkus and Padesky (1984) and by Lester, Leitner, and Posner (1984) underscored the need for such stress management programs to go beyond the individual police officer to include his or her spouse, peer counseling, and organizational and administrative changes. In the same vein, Reiser and Geiger (1984) discussed the potential role of stress management training for police officers who have been victims of physical and psychological violence. They note that organizational policies that provide support and a referral network, keep postviolence interviews short, adopt a helpful rather than adversarial attitude, communicate an awareness that victimization is traumatic for everyone, and convey the idea that unpleasant thoughts and feelings are not abnormal reactions, provide light duty assignments that allow a gradual reentry, and indicate that management and peers do care, can each help police officers cope more adequately with the stress of being a victim. Thus, teaching coping skills to police officers represents only one side of stress mangement interventions. SIT needs to include group and organizational processes as well.

Teachers

Teachers are another occupational group who have received SIT training. In an innovative series of studies, Forman (1982, 1983) extended SIT training to urban secondary school teachers. The training consisted of six

2- to 3-hour sessions once a week for 6 weeks. Training consisted of four components: presentation of conceptual framework, relaxation training, cognitive restructuring, and rehearsal-application. Following introductions and a general discussion of the definition, incidence, cause, and effects of stress on teachers and students, the discussion focused on specific school-related stressful situations (e.g., acting-out students, students who did not care about grades, time constraints, lack of resources, problems with mainstreaming, and problems with school administrators). Following relaxation and cognitive restructuring, the participants developed "stress scripts" that were constructive coping plans to deal with a variety of stressful situations. For example, one stressful scenario involved a student belligerently refusing to do a classroom assignment. The stress script focused on the automatic thoughts and feelings a stressed teacher might have in this situation and the alternative, incompatible, stress-reducing automatic thoughts or cognitive events, such as the following:

Stress-producing	*Stress-reducing*
How could he say this to me?	I want to know why he said that, so I guess I can talk to him about it.
He's getting me really upset.	I can stay calm if I want to because I control how I feel. I can relax and then I'll be able to solve this problem better.

Role-playing and imagery rehearsal were used as practice aids. Relative to control groups, the SIT resulted in decreased self-reported anxiety and stress at posttest and at a 6-week follow-up, as well as a decrease in motoric manifestations of anxiety in the classroom.

The Forman demonstration studies bear careful replication and extension. Recent attempts at stress management with teachers have been extended to include not only teachers, but also combined meetings with teachers, supervisors, principals, and/or administrators, in order to discuss and work through the impact of work-related policies (school closings, layoffs, school violence, bureaucratic decisions, and unnecessary paperwork). See Turk et al. (1982) for a discussion of the multiple sources of teacher stress. They note that efforts at stress prevention and management require interventions that go well beyond the teachers themselves.

Athletes

The need to focus on significant others besides the "target" population is also illustrated in work with athletes. With reference to the recent Los Angeles Olympic games in mind, a recurrent question has been, "What do sport psychologists have to contribute to the athletes' performance?'' One possible contribution that has been offered is stress reduction or at least the teaching of athletes to use their stress constructively and not to let it hamper their performances. In recent years, SIT and closely related stress management interventions have been successfully applied to athletes.

But before we consider the specifics of such interventions, it is worth noting that another focus of stress management has been at the level of coaches. In the same way that doctors can engender stress in hospital patients, and principals can engender stress in teachers, coaches, by their style of communicating, can engender stress in athletes. Smith, Smoll, and Curtis (1979) have noted how coaches often use unclear instructions, verbal punishment, and infrequent praise, which result in a negative attitude in the athletes toward the coach, teammates, and themselves, and in turn, contribute to poorer performance. Thus, one way to reduce stress is to influence the way coaches interact with athletes. Smith et al. used a cognitive behavioral approach to teach coaches how to model and use response-specific instructions coupled with positive feedback about the athletes' performances and more generalized encouragement. However, not all researchers are as optimistic that coaches' negative style of communicating with athletes are open to change. For example, Kirschenbaum, Wittrock, Smith, and Monson (1984) used stress inoculation intervention to teach athletes how to handle criticism. Such an approach represents an important supplement to Smith's efforts at changing coaches' behaviors.

Another focus of stress management training has been to work directly with the athletes to reduce the stress related to their specific endeavors. For example, Deikis (1982) integrated SIT into didactic presentations, to teach beginning scuba divers to handle stressful underwater tasks. The SIT training was designed to engender the divers' feelings of self-confidence in their own ability to handle stressful situations. The training consisted of eight 15-minute modules that were supplemented with in vivo rehearsal in the pool (e.g., how to handle diver panic).

The most comprehensive stress management program for athletes was developed by Smith (1980). The treatment began by enlisting athletes as collaborators by means of interviews, questionnaires, and self-monitoring, to ascertain the frequency and intensity of their anxiety and tension (e.g., the night before a game or after an error). The athletes' descriptions of their stress responses laid the groundwork for the initial conceptualization phase of the nature of stress and its impact on performance. Following the initial conceptualization session, five additional training sessions were conducted, during which specific coping skills (e.g., relaxation, attentional focusing, cognitive restructuring in the form of stress-reducing mental statements) were rehearsed and then practiced during competition. The stress management program was presented as an educational program designed to teach self-control skills and *not* as a form of psychotherapy.

Some interesting features of the training included each athlete keeping an "anti-stress" log on which he or she listed stress-producing self-statements and an anti-stress substitute for each. The latter formed the basis for subsequent practice and rehearsal. Another interesting innovation was the use of Sipprelle's (1967) induced-affect procedures as a means of the athlete's developing and rehearsing a broad spectrum of coping skills. This procedure involved asking the athlete to imagine as vividly as possible a stressful situation (e.g., performing a difficult dive) and to notice the feeling elicited by the situation. The athlete was encouraged to let that feeling grow, as signs of arousal were reinforced by the trainer (e.g., "Attend to how aroused you are becoming. Notice how the feeling grows. It will grow by itself, then you can see how you can turn it off").

During this phase the trainer asked the athlete to describe his or her thoughts and feelings, and these statements were incorporated into the trainer's instructions, which were designed to further enhance the athlete's arousal. When a high level of arousal was experienced, the athlete was instructed to "turn it off" by using coping responses. Initially, relaxation training was used, followed by coping self-statements. In time, the two coping responses were integrated into a coordinated coping response. As subjects developed coping skills to deal with the intense affect aroused during training, an increased sense of self-confidence was nurtured. The goal of the induced-affect procedure was to give athletes an opportunity to manage emotional responses that were usually greater than those elicited by in vivo stressors. That is, the imagery-based stress situations and the accompanying nurturing of arousal by the trainer were reported to be more intense than what was experienced in real-life competition (Smith, 1980).

Obviously, research is needed to assess the training consequences of the induced-anxiety procedure, as well as the beneficial value of such SIT procedures on athletic competition. As Long (1980) noted in her review of stress management research with athletes, presently the results of case studies and small demonstration studies are most encouraging, but there is a pressing need for methodologically sound outcome studies. Another needed future direction involves consideration of how environmentally based interventions can be successfully integrated into stress management training directed at "target" populations.

TREATING VICTIMS OF MAJOR
STRESSFUL LIFE EVENTS

Thus far, SIT has been applied mainly to a number of medical and mental health populations and to specific occupational groups (see Table 3.1). SIT has been applied only on a limited basis to "victim" populations such as rape victims and victims of terrorist attacks (see Meichenbaum & Jaremko, 1983). It is worth speculating, however, about how SIT could be used with specific stressed groups such as individuals who have experienced cataclysmic life events, been victimized, or are experiencing a delayed stress response syndrome. These speculations are based on my own clinical experience in having worked with such stressed clients and from an informed knowledge of the literature.

First, the trainer needs to appreciate that not all stressed (e.g., bereaved) individuals need or want formal interventions. Often, natural support efforts are sufficient to aid adjustment and nurture coping. When some form of treatment is indicated, an important feature concerns its timing. After a traumatic stressor (e.g., cataclysmic event), an individual might be too numb to benefit from formal intervention, although, in some instances, stressed clients such as parents who experienced sudden infant death might benefit from the establishment of a supportive therapeutic relationship. The comment offered earlier about permitting clients to ventilate their stressful reactions at their own pace is a useful guideline. The therapist should allow clients to express and reexperience their feelings of shock, confusion, anger, depression, helplessness, fear, and anxiety. But it is important to appreciate that the reexperiencing of traumatic events in an emotional supportive environment is not in itself therapeutic. It is not just the discharge of emotions that is beneficial. The trainer can also use the clients' reexperiences as a means of achieving more adaptive appraisal of what happened to them and to help them regain a sense of self-efficacy and enhance their self-esteem.

Ayalon (1983) has described how such expression can be achieved by means of play and fantasy in cases of victimized children. A variety of verbal and nonverbal devices can be used to enable victimized children to discuss, reenact, and reappraise traumatic experiences. Group discussion, drawing pictures, role-playing helpers and victims, puppet and fantasy play have been used to facilitate such reappraisal. Ayalon advocated the use of the school and the peer group to foster coping skills.

As Horowitz and Kaltreider (1979) noted in their description of the treatment of clients suffering from stress response syndromes, treatment depends upon the therapist's (trainer, teacher, parent) establishing a "safe relationship" with clients. Within such a relationship, clients can reappraise life events and the meanings associated with them.

As Janoff-Bulman and Frieze (1983) have noted, being a victim can severely offset the assumptions and expectations clients hold about themselves and the world. The clients' belief in personal invulnerability regarding their perceptions of the world as meaningful and comprehensible, in their assumptions that other people can be trusted, and in their views of themselves as being competent and worthwhile persons, can be severely challenged. Self-questioning, feelings of insecurity, unworthiness, weakness, and perceptions of threat and danger might be evident. The world might be viewed as threatening, and the likelihood of future recurrence might be seen as high. Victimized clients often report that the way they see the world has changed in a major way. They can feel less trusting, experience feelings of fear and vulnerability, and feel that they can no longer control what happens in their lives.

SIT is designed to help victims come to terms with their shattered assumptions. In particular, the cognitive restructuring procedures are useful in helping clients reestablish a meaningful conceptual system. SIT cannot remove the pain or the loss, but it does help clients come to terms with the view that bad things can and do happen to people but that one can somehow function in spite of such losses. The SIT treatment is designed to help clients incorporate their experiences as victims. For example, clients are made aware of the fact that they tend to be sensitized to react in a stressful manner to later milder stressors, if these show parallels with the original traumatic experiences. Forewarned clients can better understand and handle such reactions. Similarly, even intrusive repetitive thoughts can be viewed as a means of seeking meaning, of trying to sort out painful events, rather than as symptoms of maladaptive behavior.

SIT is designed to help clients redefine their reactions as well as the victimization itself. Taylor and her colleagues have described several ways in which clients try to redefine stressful events so that their views of themselves and the world are not too dislodged (Taylor, Wood, & Lichtman, 1983). To redefine their stress, victims sometimes use social comparison, or they selectively focus their attention. They might compare themselves with less fortunate others; they might create hypothetical worst-world scenarios of what could have happened; they might selectively focus on one aspect of the stressful event and view it in a more favorable light; or they might manufacture normative standards of adjustment that make their own adjustment appear exceptional. In some instances, clients might even speak of benefits that occurred from their victimizing experience. In short, it is not merely that clients are victimized but also how they appraise their victimization that influences how well they will function. The challenge for both the trainer and the client is to determine when such processes are adaptive or maladaptive. When does seeing things in a positive light serve a useful purpose and when do such appraisals contribute to poor motivation and interfere with taking necessary coping actions? This is a question that the trainer needs to raise with clients in order for them to collaboratively answer. What would be the data, the personal experiments for the clients to perform in order to assess the impact of their coping efforts?

The SIT trainer can use a number of the cognitive-behavioral techniques

SIT–D*

described in previous chapters to help clients reappraise their stress. This is *not* intended to put a Pollyanaish view on clients' miseries but to help them better understand and incorporate their plight. For example, by receiving normative information or by joining victim self-help groups, clients can obtain the needed framework to better understand their reactions. For instance, one client, a widow, was deeply concerned about hearing the voice of her deceased husband calling out to her during the night. She had mentioned this to her sister-in-law, who became alarmed, which in turn reinforced the client's own doubts and concerns. The trainer provided information that such reactions were a normal part of grieving and also indicated that such experiences likely reflected that the client had had a meaningful, loving relationship with her husband. Such events should not be viewed as a harbinger of a mental breakdown, as the client suspected, but as an attempt to hold onto something very dear, very special. The trainer also referred to several examples of her husband's being away on business trips, when she had prepared dinner for him anyway. This example led to a brief discussion of how the mind can run through automatic routines or particular, well-rehearsed scripts. The widow's visions and hearing of her deceased husband's voice can be viewed as similar processes.

But even such a clinical tactic as providing clients with normative information can be a double-edged sword. Wortman (1983) reported instances where victimized clients became more distressed when they were told that their emotional reactions and their difficulties in adjusting were a normal consequence of the victimizing events. Even though the client's distress is, in fact, due to his or her victimized status, acknowledging this can sometimes make victims feel helpless and hopeless about the future. Clearly, more research is needed to determine when reassurance or cognitive reframing reduce stress and when they exacerbate stress. The SIT trainer needs to be very sensitive to the client's reactions to each clinical technique and to be ready to back off and follow the client's lead. Once again, the trainer can anticipate such reactions in the presentation of the normative information.

In summary, the trainer needs to assess the frequency, intensity, and debilitating consequences of the client's symptoms and should empathize with how disconcerting such experiences can be. The trainer then provides normative information about the occurrence of such behavior, and, finally, he or she helps the client to reappraise the meaning of her or his symptoms. Throughout, it is a very interactive, slowly paced process. The trainer is not giving a lecture on bereavement but is following the client's lead, always checking with the client for his or her reaction. The trainer might use the imaginary other client to raise the possibility of high-probability stress reactions. For instance, in the case of the widow, the trainer might say:

I don't know if this has happened to you, but I can think of other widows much like yourself who were initially reluctant, but eventually felt comfortable enough, to share what they felt were unusual experiences. Some reported that they had heard or seen their deceased husbands. Some reported that during the night they felt his presence, an unnerving experience. . . . Have you ever had such experiences?

The art of SIT training is one of timing and communication style. Although the trainer does not want to suggest symptoms to clients nor unduly alarm them, there is a point at which raising the possibility of such stress reactions is useful. This occurs usually after clients have become comfortable about sharing their experiences.

In the same way that trainers can help clients reframe symptoms, they can also follow the clients' lead in reframing their victimization. The trainer listens carefully to how clients describe their victimization, nurturing the clients' efforts at social comparison and reconstrual processes. The trainer needs to recognize the important role of reappraisal. Victimized clients often search for meaning, looking for some purpose in what has happened to them.

Finally, the trainer should be aware of other behavioral reactions clients might experience. These include self-blame and, in the case of group disasters, survival guilt. As Janoff-Bulman and Frieze (1983) noted, certain forms of self-blame might be functional following victimization, whereas other forms might be maladaptive. They distinguished a form of behavioral self-blame, which involves attributions or causal explanations assigned to some aspect of one's behavior ("I would not have been attacked if I had not been out late at night"). This implies that the cause of being a victim is due to something that is modifiable and controllable, suggesting that the client can do something to avoid future victimization. In contrast, characterological self-blame involves attributing the cause of being a victim to some enduring personality characteristic (e.g., "I am just a gullible person"). Characterological reactions are often associated with feelings of helplessness and depression, because they imply that the cause of the mishap is due to something that is unchangeable and not under one's personal control.

Brickman et al. (1982) have also drawn an important distinction that has implications for SIT. They distinguish between attributions of responsibility for a problem (who is to blame for past events) and attributions of responsibility for a solution (who is in control of future events). The SIT trainer helps clients focus their attention and energies, not on who is responsible for the victimizing event, but on their responsibility to deal with the event now that it has occurred. Instead of allowing clients to dwell on the past in a self-berating fashion, the SIT trainer nurtures a here-and-now and future-oriented, problem-solving set. As clients describe what has happened to them, the trainer must not only empathize but also carefully probe for the clients' explanations (attributions) of what happened. For, how one appraises and explains one's victimizing experience has both diagnostic and therapeutic significance.

One can use the research findings on attribution on a preventative basis as well. This was highlighted most strikingly in a recent television news broadcast when a reporter interviewed a distraught mother whose daughter had been raped. Terribly shaken, the mother, in the presence of her victimized daughter, said:

> What will happen to my daughter? She is dirty, unclean, now and forever. She is stained. I thought I could trust this place. . . . I thought I could trust her.

One cannot help but be distressed by the vicious assault of rape, but, equally, one cannot help but be concerned about the mother's statements and the implications they hold for the child's attributional processes. Those who work with families of victims and social agencies need to counsel them about the critical role their reactions play in affecting the victim's appraisal processes and adaptational capacities.

In terms of preventative efforts, it is also worth noting that great care must be taken to ensure that clients hold realistic assumptions. This was nicely illustrated by Kidder, Boell, and Moyer (1983), who reported that female rape victims who had engaged in precautionary behaviors such as taking self-defense classes, avoiding wearing provocative clothes, and being careful not to walk in certain areas often showed the most distress after a rape incident. These women's assumptions had been shattered—taking precautions did not prevent rape. As Kidder et al. noted, preventative programs must ensure that the participants maintain a realistic appraisal of the likelihood of being a victim. Although some forms of rape might be preventable, other forms are not. Prevention or treatment programs that nurture false hopes or provide an illusion of control when in fact little control is evident can make participants more vulnerable to the deleterious aftereffects of victimization if indeed a trauma occurs.

The focus of SIT is *not* limited to cognitive reappraisal. It also highlights the important role of behavioral skills training. In some instances clients try to cope with being victims by engaging in particular behavioral actions that exert environmental control and minimize the perception of invulnerability. Attempts at bolstering one's self-confidence include the client's taking courses in self-defense training or assertiveness training or nurturing social supports. Although such precautionary efforts are useful, there is an accompanying danger that a by-product of such active coping efforts is that the client will keep the issue of victimization salient.

As described in chapter 5, the SIT trainer can nurture and help train such coping skills, as well as employ a number of other techniques focused on specific stress reactions (e.g., relaxation to treat anxiety reactions, thought stoppage to treat intrusive thoughts). However, once again, caution is required before the trainer embraces any one technique. For example, in the case of thought-stoppage procedures for the treatment of intrusive thoughts, the trainer must ask whether such intrusive ideation represents an attempt by a client to work through his or her loss and pain, or does it reflect signs that coping has failed and bear treatment in its own right. It is important to remember that not all "symptoms" of stress reactions are maladaptive and need to be eliminated or avoided. The trainer has to carefully assess both the debilitating and the potentially integrating effects of a client's stress reaction before undertaking a specific form of intervention. The trainer needs to tap the client's view of the appropriateness of the treatment. The trainer needs to be frank with the client, indicating that, for some clients, flashbacks and intrusive thoughts are an attempt to better understand and incorporate what happened to them, whereas, for others, intrusive thoughts are distressing experiences that they wish to control. In short, it is not merely having stressful reactions, but also how clients appraise them, that is critical in formulating a treatment plan.

The consideration of victims of stressful life events further underscores the need for SIT to be supplemented by other familial and community-wide efforts in the recovery and readjustment process. In order to help victims, more is needed than focusing training efforts on individuals or groups of stressed clients. Societal agencies and structures also need to be altered. SIT is seen as only one piece of a comprehensive effort to help reduce and avoid the detrimental effects of stress.

References

Abelson, R. (1976). Script processing in attitude formation and decision making. In J. Carroll & J. Payne (Eds.), *Cognition and social behavior*. Hillsdale, NJ: Erlbaum.

Alkus, S., & Padesky, C. (1984). Special problems of police officers: Stress-related issues and interventions. *The Counseling Psychologist, 11*, 55–64.

Altmaier, E., Ross, S., Leary, M., & Thornbrough, M. (1982). Matching stress inoculations' treatment components to client's anxiety mode. *Journal of Counseling Psychology, 29*, 331–334.

Anderson, K., & Masur, F. (1983). Psychological preparation for invasive medical and dental procedures. *Journal of Behavioral Medicine, 6*, 1–40.

Athabasca University Student Services Orientation Guidebook. Athabasca University, Canada, 1983.

Ayalon, O. (1983). Coping with terrorism: The Israeli case. In D. Meichenbaum & M. Jaremko (Eds.), *Stress reduction and prevention*. New York: Plenum.

Bandura, A. (1977). Self-efficacy: Toward a unifying theory of behavior change. *Psychological Review, 84*, 191–215.

Barrios, B., & Shigetomi, C. (1980). Coping skills training: Potential for prevention of fears and anxieties. *Behavior Therapy, 11*, 431–439.

Beck, A. (1963). Thinking and depression: 1. Idiosyncratic content and cognitive distortions. *Archives of General Psychiatry, 9*, 324–333.

Beck, A. (1976). *Cognitive therapy and emotional disorders*. New York: International Universities Press.

Beck, A. (1984). Cognitive approaches to stress. In R. Woolfolk & P. Lehrer (Eds.), *Principles and practice of stress management*. New York: Guilford Press.

Beck, A., Rush, J., Hollon, S., & Shaw, B. (1979). *Cognitive therapy of depression*. New York: Guilford Press.

Bistline, J. L., & Frieden, F. P. (1984). Anger control: A case study of a stress inoculation treatment for a chronic aggressive patient. *Cognitive Therapy and Research, 8*, 551–556.

Breznitz, S. (1971). A study of worrying. *British Journal of Social and Clinical Psychology, 10*, 271–279.

Brickman, P., Rabinowitz, V., Karuza, J., Coates, D., Cohn, E., & Kidder, L. (1982). Models of helping and coping. *American Psychologist, 37*, 368–384.

Brown, S. (1980). Coping skills training: An evaluation of a psychoeducational program in a community mental health setting. *Journal of Counseling Psychology, 27*, 340–345.

Cohen, F. (1984). Coping. In J. Matarazzo, S. Weiss, J. Herd, N. Miller, & S. Weiss (Eds.), *Behavioral health: A handbook of health enhancement and disease prevention*. New York: John Wiley.

Cohen, R., & Ahearn, F. (1980). *Handbook for mental health care of disaster victims*. Baltimore: Johns Hopkins University Press.

Craddock, C., Cotler, S., & Jason, L. (1978). Primary prevention: Immunization of children for speech anxiety. *Cognitive Therapy and Research, 2*, 389–396.

Cragan, M., & Deffenbacher, J. (1984). Anxiety management training and relaxation as self-control in the treatment of generalized anxiety in medical outpatients. *Journal of Counseling Psychology, 31*, 123–131.

Davidson, P. (1976). Therapeutic compliance. *Canadian Psychological Review, 17,* 247–259.

Deffenbacher, J., & Hahloser, R. (1981). Cognitive and relaxation coping skills in stress-inoculation. *Cognitive Therapy and Research, 5,* 211–215.

Deikis, J. (1982). *Stress inoculation training: Effects on anxiety, self-efficacy, and performance in divers.* Unpublished doctoral dissertation, Temple University.

Denicola, J., & Sandler, J. (1980). Training abusive parents in child management and self-control skills. *Behavior Therapy, 11,* 263–270.

DiMatteo, M., & DiNicola, D. (1982). *Achieving patient compliance.* New York: Pergamon Press.

Dinner, R., & Gal, R. (1983). Stress-inoculation training and Israeli defense airborne soldiers. Unpublished manuscript, Department of Behavioral Sciences, Israeli Defense Forces, Israel.

Dunbar, J. (1980). Adhering to medical advice: A review. *International Journal of Mental Health, 9,* 70–87.

D'Zurilla, T., & Nezu, A. (1982). Social problem-solving in adults. In D. Kendall (Ed.), *Advances in cognitive-behavioral research and therapy* (Vol. 1). New York: Academic Press.

Egan, K. (1983). Stress management and child management with abusive parents. *Journal of Clinical Child Psychology, 12,* 292–299.

Ellis, A. (1962). *Reason and emotion in psychotherapy.* New York: Lyle Stuart.

Erdahl, J., & Blythe, B. (1984). Single-case evaluation of stress inoculation training to prepare a cardiac patient for open-heart surgery. Paper presented at the meeting of the National Association of Social Work Health Conference, Washington, DC.

Feindler, E., & Fremouw, W. (1983). Stress inoculation training for adolescent anger problems. In D. Meichenbaum & M. Jaremko (Eds.), *Stress reduction and prevention.* New York: Plenum.

Feindler, E., Marriott, S., & Iwata, M. (1984). Group anger control training for junior high school dropouts. *Cognitive Therapy and Research, 8,* 299–311.

Flavell, J. (1979). Metacognition and cognitive monitoring. A new area of cognitive-developmental inquiry. *American Psychologist, 34,* 906–911.

Folkman, S. (1984). Personal control and stress and coping processes: A theoretical analysis. *Journal of Personality and Social Psychology, 46,* 839–852.

Forman, S. (1981). Stress management training: Evaluation of effects on school psychological services. *Journal of School Psychology, 19,* 233–241.

Forman, S. (1982). Stress management for teachers: A cognitive-behavioral program. *Journal of School Psychology, 20,* 180–187.

Forman, S. (1983). Occupational stress management: Cognitive-behavioral approaches. *Children and Youth Services Review, 5,* 277–287.

Frank, J. (1974). *Persuasion and healing.* New York: Schocken.

Frankenhaeuser, M. (1981). Coping with stress at work. *International Journal of Health Services, 11,* 491–570.

Fremouw, W., & Harmatz, M. (1975). A helper model for behavioral treatment of speech anxiety. *Journal of Consulting and Clinical Psychology, 43,* 652–660.

Fremouw, W., & Zitter, R. (1978). A comparison of skills training and cognitive restructuring-relaxation for the treatment of speech anxiety. *Behavior Therapy, 9,* 248–259.

Gaertner, G., Craighead, L., & Horan, J. (1983). *A component analysis of stress inoculation applied to institutionalized public offenders with anger and aggression management deficiencies.* Unpublished manuscript, Pennsylvania State University.

Genest, M. (1979). *A cognitive-behavioral bibliotherapy to ameliorate pain.* Unpublished master's thesis. University of Waterloo, Ontario, Canada.

Girodo, M., & Roehl, J. (1978). Cognitive preparation and coping self-talk: Anxiety management during the stress of flying. *Journal of Consulting and Clinical Psychology, 46,* 978–989.

Girodo, M., & Wood, D. (1979). Talking yourself out of pain: The importance of believing you can. *Cognitive Therapy and Research, 3,* 23–33.

Glass, C., Gottman, J., & Shmurak, S. (1976). Response acquisition and cognitive self-statement modification approaches to dating skill training. *Journal of Counseling Psychology,* 23, 520–526.

Goldfried, M. (1971). Systematic desensitization as training in self-control. *Journal of Consulting and Clinical Psychology, 37,* 228–234.

Goldfried, M. (1977). The use of relaxation and cognitive relabeling as coping skills. In R. Stuart (Ed.), *Behavioral self-management: Strategies, techniques and outcomes.* New York: Brunner/Mazel.

Goldfried, M. (1979). Psychotherapy as coping skills training. In M. Mahoney (Ed.), *Psychotherapy process: Current issues and future directions.* New York: Plenum.

Goldfried, M., & Davison, G. (1976). *Clinical behavior therapy.* New York: Holt, Rinehart and Winston.

Goldfried, M., Decenteceo, E., & Weinberg, L. (1974). Systematic rational restructuring as a self-control technique. *Behavior Therapy, 5,* 247–254.

Goldfried, M., & D'Zurilla, T. (1969). A behavior-analytic model for assessment of competence. In C. Spielberger (Ed.), *Current topics in clinical and community psychology.* New York: Academic Press.

Goldfried, M., & Goldfried, A. (1980). Cognitive change methods. In F. Kanfer & A. Goldstein (Eds.), *Helping people change.* New York: Pergamon Press.

Hackett, G., & Horan, J. (1980). Stress inoculation for pain: What's really going on? *Journal of Counseling Psychology, 27,* 107–116.

Hackett, G., Horan, J., Buchanan, J., & Zumoff, P. (1979). Improving exposure component and generalization potential of stress inoculation for pain. *Perceptual and Motor Skills, 48,* 1132–1134.

Heppner, P., Neal, G., & Larsen, L. (1984). Problem-solving training as prevention with college students. *Personnel and Guidance Journal, 62,* 514–519.

Holcomb, W. (1979). *Coping with severe stress: A clinical application of stress inoculation therapy.* Unpublished doctoral dissertation, University of Missouri-Columbia.

Hollon, S., & Beck, A. (1979). Cognitive therapy of depression. In S. Hollon & P. Kendall (Eds.), *Cognitive-behavioral interventions: Therapy, research and procedures.* New York: Academic Press.

Holroyd, K., & Andrasik, F. (1978). Coping and the self-control of chronic tension headache. *Journal of Consulting and Clinical Psychology, 46,* 1036–1045.

Holroyd, K., Andrasik, F., & Westbrook, T. (1977). Cognitive control of tension headache. *Cognitive Therapy and Research, 1,* 121–133.

Holroyd, K., Pensien, D., Hursey, K., Tobin, D., Rogers, L., Holm, J., Marcelle, P., Hall, J., & Chila, A. (in press). Change mechanisms in EMG biofeedback training: Cognitive changes underlying improvements in tension headache. *Journal of Consulting and Clinical Psychology.*

Horan, J., Hackett, G., Buchanan, J., Stone, C., & Demchik-Stone, D. (1977). Coping with pain: A component analysis of stress inoculation. *Cognitive Therapy and Research, 1,* 211–221.

Horney, K. (1950). *Neurosis and human growth: The struggle toward self-realization.* New York: W.W. Norton.

Horowitz, M., & Kaltreider, N. (1979). Brief psychotherapy of stress response syndromes. In T. Karasu & L. Bellack (Eds.), *Specialized techniques in individual psychotherapy.* New York: Brunner/Mazel.

Hussain, R., & Lawrence, P. (1978). The reduction of test, state and trait anxiety by test-specific and generalized stress inoculation training. *Cognitive Therapy and Research, 2,* 25–37.

Janis, I. (1958). *Psychological stress.* New York: John Wiley.

Janis, I., & Mann, L. (1977). *Decision making.* New York: Free Press.

Janoff-Bulman, R., & Frieze, I. (1983). A theoretical perspective for understanding reactions to victimization. *Journal of Social Issues, 39,* 1–17.

Jaremko, M. (1979). A component analysis of stress inoculation: Review and prospectus.

Cognitive Therapy and Research, 3, 35–48.

Jaremko, M. (1980). The use of stress inoculation training in the reduction of public speaking anxiety. *Journal of Clinical Psychology, 36,* 735–738.

Jaremko, M. (1983). Stress inoculation training for social anxiety, with emphasis on dating anxiety. In D. Meichenbaum & M. Jaremko (Eds.), *Stress reduction and prevention.* New York: Plenum.

Jaremko, M., Hadfield, R., & Walker, W. (1980). Contribution of an educational phase to stress inoculation of speech anxiety. *Perceptual and Motor Skills, 50,* 495–501.

Jason, L., & Burrows, B. (1983). Transition training for high school seniors. *Cognitive Therapy and Research, 7,* 79–92.

Jenni, M., & Wollersheim, J. (1979). Cognitive therapy, stress management, and the Type A behavior pattern. *Cognitive Therapy and Research, 3,* 61–73.

Jorgensen, R., Houston, B., & Zurawski, R. (1981). Anxiety management training in the treatment of essential hypertension. *Behaviour Research and Therapy, 19,* 467–474.

Kantor, L. (1978). *Stress-inoculation as a means of teaching anxiety management skills.* Unpublished doctoral dissertation, Bowling Green State University.

Karol, K., Doerfler, L., Parker, J., & Armentraut, D. (1981). A therapist manual for the cognitive-behavioral treatment of chronic pain. *JSAS Catalogue of Selected Documents in Psychology, 11,* 15–61. (Ms. No. 2205).

Kazdin, A. (1973). Covert modeling and the reduction of avoidance behavior. *Journal of Abnormal Psychology, 81,* 87–95.

Kelley, H., & Stahelski, A. (1970). Errors in perception of intentions in a mixed-motive game. *Journal of Experimental Social Psychology, 6,* 370–400.

Kendall, P. (1983). Stressful medical procedures: Cognitive-behavioral strategies for stress management and prevention. In D. Meichenbaum & M. Jaremko, *Stress reduction and prevention.* New York: Plenum.

Kendall, P., & Bemis, K. (1983). Thought and action in psychotherapy: The cognitive-behavioral approaches. In M. Hersen, A. Kazdin, & A. Bellack (Eds.), *The clinical psychology handbook.* New York: Pergamon Press.

Kendall, P., Williams, L., Pechacek, T., Graham, L., Sisslak, C., & Herzoff, N. (1979). Cognitive-behavioral and patient education interventions in cardiac catherization procedures: The Palo Alto medical psychology project. *Journal of Consulting and Clinical Psychology, 47,* 49–58.

Kendrick, M. (1979). *Reduction of musical performance anxiety by attentional training and behavioral rehearsal: An exploration of cognitive medicational processes.* Unpublished doctoral dissertation, University of British Columbia.

Kessler, R., Price, R., & Wortman, C. (in press). Social and cultural influences on psychopathology. *Annual Review of Psychology.* Palo Alto: California.

Kidder, L., Boell, J., & Moyer, M. (1983). Rights, consciousness and victimization prevention. Personal defense and assertiveness training. *Journal of Social Issues, 39,* 153–168.

Kirschenbaum, D., Wittrock, D., Smith, R., & Monson, W. (1984). Criticism inoculation training. *Journal of Sport Psychology, 6,* 77–93.

Klepac, R., Hague, G., Dowling, J., & McDonald, M. (1981). Direct and generalized effects of three components of stress inoculation for increased pain tolerance. *Behavior Therapy, 12,* 417–424.

Klinger, E. (1977). *Meaning and void: inner experience and the incentives in people's lives.* Minneapolis: University of Minnesota Press.

Klinger, E., Barta, S., & Maxeiner, M. (1981). Current concerns: Assessing therapeutically relevant motivation. In P. Kendall & S. Hollon (Eds.), *Assessment strategies for cognitive-behavioral interventions.* New York: Academic Press.

Lang, P. (1968). Fear reduction and fear behavior. Problems in treating a construct. In J. Shlien

(Ed.), *Research in Psychotherapy* (Vol. 3). Washington, DC: American Psychological Association.

Langer, T., Janis, I., & Wolfer, J. (1975). Reduction of psychological stress in surgical patients. *Journal of Experimental Social Psychology, 11*, 155–165.

Lazarus, R. (1975). A cognitively oriented psychologist looks at biofeedback. *American Psychologist, 30*, 553–560.

Lazarus, R. (1981). The stress and coping paradigm. In C. Eisdorfer (Ed.), *Models for clinical psychopathology*. Englewood Cliffs, NJ: Prentice-Hall.

Lazarus, R. (1984). The costs and benefits of denial. In S. Breznitz (Ed.), *Denial of stress*. New York: International Universities Press.

Lazarus, R., & Folkman, S. (1984). *Stress, appraisal and coping*. New York: Springer.

Lazarus, R., & Launier, R. (1978). Stress-related transactions between persons and environment. In L. Pervin & M. Lewis (Eds.), *Perspectives in interactional psychology*. New York: Plenum.

Lester, D., Leitner, C., & Posner, I. (1984). The effects of a stress management training programme on police officers. *International Review of Applied Psychology, 33*, 25–31.

Levendusky, P., & Pankratz, L. (1975). Self-control techniques as an alternative to pain medication. *Journal of Abnormal Psychology, 85*, 165–168.

Leventhal, H., Meyer, D., & Nerenz, D. (1980). The common sense representation of illness. In S. Rachman (Ed.), *Medical Psychology* (Vol. 2). London: Pergamon Press.

Linehan, M., & Egan, K. (1983). *Asserting yourself*. Toronto: John Wiley.

Long, B. (1980). Stress management for the athlete: A cognitive behavioral model. In C. Nadeau, W. Halliwell, K. Newell, & G. Roberts (Eds.), *Psychology of Motor Behavior and Sport—1979*. Champaign, IL: Human Kinetics.

Long, B. (1982). *A comparison of aerobic conditioning and stress inoculation as stress-management interventions*. Unpublished doctoral dissertation, University of British Columbia.

Long, B. (1984). Aerobic conditioning and stress inoculation: A comparison of stress-management interventions. *Cognitive Therapy and Research, 5*, 517–542.

Long, B. (in press a). Stress-management interventions: A 15-month follow-up of aerobic conditioning and stress-inoculation training. *Cognitive Therapy and Research*.

Luborsky, L., & De Rubeis, R. (1984). The use of psychotherapy treatment manuals: A small revolution in psychotherapy research style. *Clinical Psychology Review, 4*, 5–14.

MacDonald, M., & Kuiper, N. (1983). Cognitive-behavioral preparations for surgery. *Clinical Psychology Review, 3*, 27–39.

Mahoney, M. (1977). Personal science: A cognitive learning therapy. In A. Ellis & R. Grieger (Eds.), *Handbook of rational-emotive therapy*. New York: Springer.

Mahoney, M. (1982). Psychotherapy and human change processes. In J. Harvey & M. Parke (Eds.), *Psychotherapy research and behavior change*. Washington, DC: American Psychological Association.

Markus, H. (1977). Self-schemata and processing information about the self. *Journal of Personality and Social Psychology, 35*, 63–78.

Marlatt, A., & Gordon, J. (1984). *Relapse prevention: A self-control strategy for the maintenance of behavior change*. New York: Guilford Press.

Marmor, J. (1958). The psychodynamics of realistic worry. *Psychoanalysis and Social Science, 5*, 155–163.

Mason, J. (1975). An historical view of the stress field. *Journal of Human Stress, 1*, 6–12.

McCaffery, M. (1979). *Nursing management of the patient with pain*. Philadelphia: J.B. Lippincott.

Meichenbaum, D. (1971). Examination of model characteristics in reducing avoidance behavior. *Journal of Personality and Social Psychology, 17*, 298–307.

Meichenbaum, D. (1972). Cognitive modification of test anxious college students. *Journal of Consulting and Clinical Psychology, 39*, 370–380.

Meichenbaum, D. (1976). Cognitive factors in biofeedback therapy. *Biofeedback and self-regulation, 1,* 201–216.

Meichenbaum, D. (1977). *Cognitive-behavior modification: An integrative approach.* New York: Plenum.

Meichenbaum, D. (1978). Why does using imagery in psychotherapy lead to change? In J. Singer & K. Pope (Eds.), *The power of human imagination.* New York: Plenum.

Meichenbaum, D. (1983). *Coping with stress.* Toronto: John Wiley.

Meichenbaum, D., & Cameron, R. (1972). *Stress inoculation: A skills training approach to anxiety management.* Unpublished manuscript, University of Waterloo.

Meichenbaum, D., & Gilmore, J. (1984). The nature of unconscious processes: A cognitive-behavioral perspective. In K. Bowers & D. Meichenbaum (Eds.), *The unconscious reconsidered.* New York: John Wiley.

Meichenbaum, D., Henshaw, D., & Himel, N. (1982). Coping with stress as a problem-solving process. In W. Krohne & L. Laux (Eds.), *Achievement, stress and anxiety.* Washington, DC: Hemisphere Press.

Meichenbaum, D., & Jaremko, M. (1983). *Stress reduction and prevention.* New York: Plenum.

Meichenbaum, D., & Novaco, R. (1978). Stress inoculation: A preventative approach. In C. Spielberger & I. Sarason (Eds.), *Stress and Anxiety* (Vol. 5). New York: Halsted Press.

Melamed, B. (1982). Reduction of medical fears: An information processing analysis. In J. Boulougouris (Ed.), *Learning theory approaches to psychiatry.* New York: John Wiley.

Melamed, B., & Siegel, L. (1975). Reduction of anxiety in children facing hospitalization and surgery by use of filmed modeling. *Journal of Consulting and Clinical Psychology, 43,* 511–521.

Melzack, R., & Wall, P. (1965). Pain mechanism: A new theory. *Science, 150,* 971–974.

Moore, K., & Altmaier, E. (1981). Stress inoculation training with cancer patients. *Cancer Nursing, 10,* 389–393.

Moos, R. (1974). *Evaluating treatment environments: A social ecological approach.* New York: John Wiley.

Neisser, U. (1976). *Cognition and reality: Principles and implications of cognitive psychology.* San Francisco: Freeman, Cooper.

Nelson, R. (1977). Assessment and therapeutic functions of self-monitoring. In M. Hersen, R. Eisler, & P. Miller (Eds.), *Progress in behavior modification.* (Vol. 5). New York: Academic Press.

Nisbett, R., & Ross, L. (1980). *Human inference: Strategies and shortcomings of social judgment.* Englewood Cliffs, NJ: Prentice-Hall.

Novaco, R. (1975). *Anger control: The development and evaluation of an experimental treatment.* Lexington, MA: D.C. Heath.

Novaco, R. (1977a). Stress inoculation: A cognitive therapy for anger and its application to a case of depression. *Journal of Consulting and Clinical Psychology, 45,* 600–608.

Novaco, R. (1977b). A stress inoculation approach to anger management in the training of law enforcement officers. *American Journal of Community Psychology, 5,* 327–346.

Novaco, R. (1980). Training of probation officers for anger problems. *Journal of Counseling Psychology, 27,* 385–390.

Novaco, R., Cook, T., & Sarason, I. (1983). Military recruit training: An arena for stress-coping skills. In D. Meichenbaum & M. Jaremko (Eds.), *Stress reduction and prevention.* New York: Plenum.

Nye, S. (1979). *Self-instructional stress management training: A comparison of the effects of induced affect and covert modeling in a cognitive restructuring treatment program for test anxiety.* Unpublished doctoral dissertation, University of Washington.

Orne, M. (1965). Psychological factors maximizing resistance to stress with special reference to hypnosis. In S. Klausner (Ed.), *The quest for self-control.* New York: Free Press.

Pearlin, L., & Schooler, C. (1978). The structure of coping. *Journal of Health and Social Behavior, 19,* 2–21.

Poser, E. (1976). Strategies for behavioral prevention. In P. O. Davidson (Ed.), *The behavioral management of anxiety, depression and pain*. New York: Brunner/Mazel.

Poser, E., & King, M. (1975). Strategies for the prevention of maladaptive fear responses. *Canadian Journal of Behavioral Sciences, 7*, 279–294.

Poser, E., & King, M. (1976). Primary prevention of fear: An experimental approach. In I. Sarason & C. Spielberger (Eds.), *Stress and anxiety* (Vol. 3). Washington, DC: Hemisphere Press.

Quillen, M., & Denney, D. (1982). Self-control of dysmenorrhea symptoms through pain management training. *Journal of Behavior Therapy and Experimental Psychiatry, 11*, 229–232.

Raimy, V. (1975). *Misunderstanding of the self: Cognitive psychotherapy and the misconception hypothesis*. San Francisco: Jossey-Bass.

Randich, S. (1982). *Evaluation of stress inoculation training as a pain management program for rheumatoid arthritis*. Unpublished doctoral dissertation, Washington University, St. Louis.

Reiser, M., & Geiger, S. (1984). Police officer as victim. *Professional Psychology: Research and Practice, 15*, 315–323.

Robin, A. (1981). A controlled evaluation of problem-solving communication training with parent-adolescent conflict. *Behavior Therapy, 12*, 593–609.

Rodin, J. (Speaker). (1979). *Cognitive behavior therapy for obesity* (Cassette Recording No. 1). New York: BMA Audio Cassettes.

Rodin, J. (1983). *Controlling your weight*. Toronto: John Wiley.

Roskies, E. (1983). Stress management for Type A individuals. In D. Meichenbaum & M. Jaremko (Eds.), *Stress prevention and reduction*. New York: Plenum.

Rush, J. (1983). *Beating depression*. Toronto: John Wiley.

Rybstein-Blinchik, E. (1979). Effects of different cognitive strategies on chronic pain experience. *Journal of Behavioral Medicine, 2*, 93–105.

Salovey, P., & Haar, M. D. (1983, April). Treating writing anxiety: Cognitive restructuring and writing process training. Paper presented at the annual meeting of the American Educational Research Association, Montreal, Canada.

Sarason, I. (1975). Anxiety and self-preoccupation. In I. Sarason & C. Spielberger (Eds.), *Stress and Anxiety* (Vol. 2). Washington, DC: Hemisphere Press.

Sarason, I., Johnson, J., Berberich, J., & Siegel, J. (1979). Helping police officers to cope with stress: A cognitive-behavioral approach. *American Journal of Community Psychology, 7*, 593–603.

Schachter, S. (1966). The interaction of cognitive and physiological determinants of emotion. In C. Spielberger (Ed.), *Anxiety and behavior*. New York: Academic Press.

Schlichter, K., & Horan, J. (1981). Effects of stress inoculation on the anger and aggression management skills in institutionalized juvenile delinquents. *Cognitive Therapy and Research, 4*, 359–365.

Selye, H. (1974). *Stress without distress*. Philadelphia: J. B. Lippincott.

Shaw, E., & Blanchard, E. (1983). The effects of instructional set on the outcome of a stress management program. *Biofeedback and self-regulation, 8*, 555–566.

Shelton, J., & Ackerman, J. (1974). *Homework in counseling and psychotherapy*. Springfield, IL: Charles C. Thomas.

Siegel, L., & Peterson, L. (1980). Stress reduction in young dental patients through coping skills and sensory information. *Journal of Consulting and Clinical Psychology, 48*, 785–787.

Silver, R., & Wortman, C. (1980). Coping with undesirable life events. In J. Garber & M. Seligman (Eds.), *Human helplessness: Theory and applications*. New York: Academic Press.

Sipprelle, C. (1967). Induced anxiety. *Psychotherapy: Theory, Research and Practice, 4*, 36–40.

Smith, R. (1980). A cognitive-affective approach to stress management training for athletes. In C. Nadeau, W. Halliwell, K. Newell, & G. Roberts (Eds.), *Psychology of Motor Behavior and Sport—1979*. Champaign, IL: Human Kinetics.

Smith, R., Smoll, F., & Curtis, B. (1979). Coach effectiveness training: A cognitive-behavioural approach to enhancing relationship skills in youth sport coaches. *Journal of Sport Psychology,* *1,* 59–75.

Smoll, F., & Smith, R. (1980). Psychologically oriented coach training programs: Design, implementation and assessment. In C. Nadeau, W. Halliwell, K. Newell, & G. Roberts (Eds.), *Psychology of motor behavior and sport—1979.* Champaign, IL: Human Kinetics.

Snyder, M. (1981). Seek, and ye shall find: Testing hypotheses about other people. In E. Higgins, C. Herman, & M. Zanna (Eds.), *Social Cognition: The Ontario symposium.* Hillsdale, NJ: Erlbaum.

Sobel, H., & Worden, J. (1981). *Helping cancer patients cope: A problem-solving intervention for health care professionals.* New York: BMA and Guilford Press.

Strupp, H., & Binder, J. (1982). *Time limited dynamic psychotherapy: A treatment manual.* Unpublished manuscript, Vanderbilt University.

Suinn, R. (1977). *Manual: Anxiety management training.* Fort Collins, CO: Rocky Mountain Behavioral Science Institute.

Suinn, R. (1982). Intervention with Type A behaviors. *Journal of Consulting and Clinical Psychology, 50,* 933–949.

Suinn, R., & Richardson, F. (1971). Anxiety management training. A non-specific behavior therapy program for anxiety control. *Behavior Therapy, 2,* 498–510.

Sweeney, G., & Horan, J. (1982). Separate and combined effects of uncontrolled relaxation and cognitive restructuring in the treatment of musical performance anxiety. *Journal of Counseling Psychology, 29,* 486–497.

Tableman, B., Marciniak, D., Johnson, D., & Rodgers, R. (1982). Stress management training for women on public assistance. *American Journal of Community Psychology, 10,* 357–367.

Taylor, S., & Crocker, J. (1981). Schematic bases of social information processing. In E. Higgins, C. Herman, & M. Zanna (Eds.), *Social cognition: The Ontario symposium.* Hillsdale, NJ: Erlbaum.

Taylor, S., Wood, J., & Lichtman, R. (1983). It could be worse: Selective evaluation as a response to victimization. *Journal of Social Issues, 39,* 19–40.

Thurman, C. (1984). Cognitive-behavioral interventions with Type A faculty. *Personnel and Guidance Journal, 2,* 358–362.

Turk, D. (1977). *A coping skills approach for the control of experimentally produced pain.* Unpublished doctoral dissertation, University of Waterloo, Ontario.

Turk, D., Holzman, A., & Kerns, R. (1985). Treatment of chronic pain: Emphasis on self-management. In K. Holroyd & T. Creer (Eds.), *Self-management in health psychology and behavioral medicine.* New York: Academic Press.

Turk, D., Meeks, S., & Turk, L. (1982). Factors contributing to teacher stress: Implications for research prevention and remediation. *Behavioral Counseling Quarterly, 2,* 3–25.

Turk, D., Meichenbaum, D., & Genest, M. (1983). *Pain and behavioral medicine.* New York: Guilford Press.

Turk, D., & Speers, M. (1983). Cognitive schemata and cognitive processes in cognitive behavior modification: Going beyond the information given. In P. Kendall (Ed.), *Advances in cognitive-behavioral research and therapy* (Vol. 2). New York: Academic Press.

Tversky, A., & Kahneman, D. (1977). Causal schemata in judgments under uncertainty. In M. Fishbein (Ed.), *Progress in social psychology.* Hillsdale, NJ: Erlbaum.

Twentyman, C., Rohrbeck, C., & Amish, P. (1984). A cognitive-behavioral model of child abuse. In S. Saunders (Ed.), *Violent individuals and families: A practitioner's handbook.* Springfield, IL: Charles C. Thomas.

Ulissi, S. (1978). *The efficacy of stress inoculation training and induced anxiety.* Unpublished doctoral dissertation, University of Mississippi.

Vallis, T. (1984). A complete component analysis of stress inoculation for pain tolerance. *Cognitive Therapy and Research, 8,* 313–330.

Varni, J., Jay, S., Masek, B., & Thompson, K. (in press). Cognitive-behavioral assessment and management of pediatric pain. In A. Holzman & D. Turk (Eds.), *Pain management: A handbook of psychological treatment approaches.* New York: Pergamon Press.

Veronen, L., & Kilpatrick, D. (1983). Stress management for rape victims. In D. Meichenbaum & M. Jaremko (Eds.), *Stress reduction and prevention.* New York: Plenum.

Volicer, B., & Bohannon, M. (1975). A hospital stress rating scale. *Nursing Research, 24,* 352–359.

Wachtel, P. (1977). *Psychoanalysis and behavior therapy.* New York: Basic Books.

Wachtel, P. (1982). What can dynamic therapies contribute to behavior therapy? *Behavior Therapy, 13,* 594–609.

Wasik, B. (1984). *Teaching parents effective problem-solving: A handbook for professionals.* Unpublished manuscript. University of North Carolina, Chapel Hill.

Waterhouse, G., & Strupp, H. (1984). The patient-therapist relationship: Research from the psychodynamic perspective. *Clinical Psychology Review, 4,* 77–92.

Weiner, B. (1972). *Theories of motivation.* Chicago: Markham.

Weisman, A., Worden, J., & Sobel, H. (1980). *Psychosocial screening and intervention with cancer patients.* Unpublished manuscript, Harvard Medical School.

Wernick, R. (1983). Stress inoculation in the management of clinical pain: Applications to burn pain. In D. Meichenbaum & M. Jaremko (Eds.), *Stress reduction and prevention.* New York: Plenum.

Wernick, R. (1984). Stress management with practical nursing students: Effects on attrition. *Cognitive Therapy and Research, 8,* 543–550.

Wernick, R., Jaremko, M., & Taylor, P. (1981). Pain management in severely burned adults: A test of stress inoculation. *Journal of Behavioral Medicine, 4,* 103–109.

West, D., Horan, J., & Games, P. (1984). Component analysis of occupational stress inoculation applied to registered nurses in an acute care hospital setting. *Journal of Counseling Psychology, 31,* 209–218.

Wolpe, J. (1959). *Psychotherapy by reciprocal inhibition.* Stanford, CA: Stanford University Press.

Woolfolk, R., & Lehrer, P. (1984). *Principles and practice of stress management.* New York: Guilford Press.

Worthington, E. (1978). The effects of imagery content, choice of imagery, and self-verbalization on the self-control of pain. *Cognitive Therapy and Research, 2,* 225–239.

Worthington, E., & Shumate, M. (1981). Imagery and verbal counseling methods in stress inoculation training for pain control. *Journal of Counseling Psychology, 28,* 1–6.

Wortman, C. (1983). Coping with victimization: Conclusions and implications for future research. *Journal of Social Issues, 39,* 195–221.

Author Index

Subject Index

About the Author

Donald Meichenbaum, Ph.D. is one of the founders of Cognitive Behavior Modification (CBM), and his 1977 book, *Cognitive Behavior Modification: An Integrative Approach* is considered a classic in the field. He has also authored *Coping With Stress*, coauthored *Pain and Behavioral Medicine*, and coedited *Stress Reduction and Prevention* and *The Unconscious Reconsidered*. He is associate editor of *Cognitive Therapy and Research* and is on the editorial boards of a dozen journals. He is currently Professor of Psychology at the University of Waterloo, Waterloo, Ontario, Canada, a clinical psychologist in private practice, and has served as a consultant to psychiatric, medical, educational, correctional and business institutions.

In a recent survey reported in the *American Psychologist*, North American clinicians voted Dr. Meichenbaum one of the ten most influential psychotherapists of the century. He has presented workshops and lectures throughout the United States, Canada, Europe, Israel and Russia.

Pergamon Psychology Practitioner Guidebook Series

Editors:
Arnold P. Goldstein, Syracuse University
Leonard Krasner, SUNY at Stony Brook
Sol L. Garfield, Washington University

Edward B. Blanchard & Frank Andrasik – *MANAGEMENT OF CHRONIC HEADACHES: A Psychological Approach*

Philip H. Bornstein & Marcy T. Bornstein – *MARITAL THERAPY: A Behavioral-Communications Approach*

Karen S. Calhoun & Beverly M. Atkeson – *TREATMENT OF VICTIMS OF SEXUAL ASSAULT*

Richard F. Dangel & Richard A. Polster – *TEACHING CHILD MANAGEMENT SKILLS*

Eva L. Feindler & Randolph B. Ecton – *ADOLESCENT ANGER CONTROL: Cognitive-Behavioral Techniques*

Paul Karoly & Mark P. Jensen – *CLINICAL PAIN ASSESSMENT*

Donald Meichenbaum – *STRESS INOCULATION TRAINING*

Michael T. Nietzel & Ronald C. Dillehay – *PSYCHOLOGICAL CONSULTATION IN THE COURTROOM*

Elsie M. Pinkston & Nathan L. Linsk – *CARE OF THE ELDERLY: A Family Approach*

Alice W. Pope, Susan M. McHale & W. Edward Craighead – *SELF-ESTEEM ENHANCEMENT WITH CHILDREN AND ADOLESCENTS*

Raymond G. Romanczyk – *CLINICAL UTILIZATION OF MICRO-COMPUTER TECHNOLOGY*

Sebastiano Santostefano – *COGNITIVE CONTROL THERAPY WITH CHILDREN AND ADOLESCENTS*

Lillie Weiss, Melanie Katzman & Sharlene Wolchik – *TREATING BULIMIA: A Psychoeducational Approach*

Elizabeth Yost, Larry E. Beutler, Anne Corbishley & James Allender – *GROUP COGNITIVE THERAPY: A Treatment Method for the Depressed Elderly*